THE BIGGEST FISH EVER CAUGHT

A Long String

of (Mostly)

True

Stories

ANDREW VIETZE

LYONS PRESS
Guilford, Connecticut
An imprint of Globe Pequot Press

Lyons Press is an imprint of Globe Pequot Press.

Photos on pp. 7, 17, 26, 40, 59, 72, 85, 96, 105, 128, and 148 licensed by
Shutterstock.com.

Project editor: Staci Zacharski
Text design: Linda Loiewski
Layout artist: Sue Murray

Library of Congress Cataloging-in-Publication Data

Vietze, Andrew.
 The biggest fish ever caught : a long string of (mostly) true stories / Andrew Vietze.
    pages cm
 Summary: "How did they do it? What are the secrets of the fishermen who've landed the
world's greatest trophy fishes? The Biggest Fish Ever Caught will tell the tales behind the
International Game Fishing Association's record-holding fish, including where they were
bagged, what lines/lures the anglers used, and other tips and tricks. The dozen stories here
are filled with amazing action and intriguing characters. They'll take you to lakes, streams,
and oceans around the world and explore catch and release vs blood sport fishing, stocking and bioengineering, conservation - and controversy. All the while revealing the sorts of
secrets fishermen don't usually like to share" — Provided by publisher.
 Includes index.
 ISBN 978-0-7627-8257-4
 1. Fishing—Records—Anecdotes. 2. Fishing—Anecdotes. 3. Fishers—Biography—
Anecdotes. I. Title.
 SH455.V54 2013
 799.1—dc23
                                                                        2013019005

Printed in the United States of America

10 9 8 7 6 5 4 3 2 1

This book is for my fishing buddies: Bruce White, Rachel Story, Marybeth and Mark, Betsy and Yves, Mike and Mike, Jennifer Smith-Mayo, Joe and Lisa McSwain, and all the other anglers who inspire me at Daicey Pond. And especially Charity and Dean Levasseur. Dean is the king of fishing in these parts as far as I can tell, offering tips, giving away flies, loaning out his boat and fly rod to complete strangers, and answering questions by the hundreds, always with patience and a genuine interest in helping out fellow anglers. They don't call him "LL Dean" for nothing.

CONTENTS

INTRODUCTION

Every fisherman has a bit of the Ahab in him. As a park ranger stationed at a popular fishing pond in Maine's North Woods, I see eager anglers on a daily basis from October to November. They come from all over the world to explore the depths of the spruce-ringed, thirty-eight-acre basin out front—and the dozen others within walking distance—for its native population of brook trout. They seek me out for fishing licenses, for keys to the boats we have on remote ponds, to ask about the rules and regulations, and sometimes for advice on where they're biting and what flies are working.

Then they head out, and I marvel at their passion and drive. They're on the water, seated in a canoe, when the rain is coming down in torrents. They're out there when the first snows of the season begin to fall softly down. They're out there when the whitecaps are blowing right over the rails into their boats. They're out there when nothing is rising, and the only things biting are thick clouds of maddening blackflies.

Nothing can stop a fisherman. The only other species that can rival their determination might be New England gardeners. Or golfers. Or adolescent video gamers. Or those blackflies. Single-minded. Focused. So in love with what they do.

It's a beautiful thing.

My dirty little secret: I'm no angler. Which isn't to say I'm not very good. I simply don't fish. Like Theodore Roosevelt, I never acquired a taste for it, always finding it a little slow. I prefer to hike and climb and paddle. People are often shocked that the ranger at Daicey Pond, surrounded by some of the finest fishing in the northeast, doesn't wet a line now and again. (And a Registered Maine Guide at that.) Some of my fellow rangers, posted mountainside or at gatehouses, want to bump me off and take my spot simply on principal.

But I have a real admiration for fishermen because they will not be deterred. If they set aside a day for fishing, they will fish, come what may, Always with the idea that on a lucky day one of them will strike it big, hauling in a monster. Perhaps it'll be big enough for the angler to contact the International Game Fish Association (IGFA) and have it considered for a record.

Based in Dania Beach, Florida, IGFA does the fishing world's bookkeeping, tracking the largest fish caught anywhere on the globe with a rod and reel. Founded by a group of deepwater fishermen in 1939, the organization was originally formed to help set ethical standards for ocean angling. Up to that point, there were no universals, and fishing clubs, countries, and individual anglers all operated on their own moral codes. This led to many disputes and record confusion, and certainly didn't help global fish populations.

In the early thirties, famed angler Michael Lerner met with British fisherman Clive Firth and discussed the idea of an international association to codify fishing standards and establish saltwater fishing records. Being a scientist, Lerner wanted to keep gamefish populations healthy as much as he wanted to keep some of the records he'd set, and IGFA's mission always included a message of conservation. The pair met with the American Museum of Natural Science, which was involved initially, and the institution's Dr. William Gregory became the first president of the nascent organization in 1939. Another well-known fisherman by the name of Ernest Hemingway lent his support and was an early officer.

Freshwater records at the time—those records held by fishing legends like Townsend Miller, George Perry, and Cal

Johnson—were kept by *Field & Stream* magazine. The association absorbed those in 1978.

To meet IGFA's standards a potential record breaker must:

- Be caught on a standard mono-, multi-, or lead-filament line with a standard rod and a reel that has no power aids.

- Fishing chairs and gaffs are allowed but again, no added power.

- Fishermen must fight the fish alone but can be helped by a gaffer and/or a friend who grabs the leader when it touches the end of the rod or is within reach of the boat.

That's it. There are many specifications and permutations—line class, hook size, line types, etc.—but that's the gist of it: a single fisherman fighting a single fish, with a little assistance in the landing acceptable when the fish is boatside.

To qualify for a record, IGFA requires a certain amount of documentation: clear photographs of the fish and the fisherman; certified weight; line and tippet samples; and name of boat, captain, weighmaster, and witnesses. The application must be notarized. For obvious reasons the process is rigorous. Some conservationists argue that it's too rigorous, that it doesn't allow anglers to catch and release a fish for fear of missing out on a record. I address this debate in the Afterword at the end of the book.

Fishermen vie for records in a multitude of line classes but the stories in this book deal with all-tackle world records (except for Stacey Parkerson's Pacific blue marlin, which is remarkable because it was caught on a fly. A fly!).

As the title says, these are the biggest fish ever caught.

BLACK PIRANHA

RUSSELL JENSEN, FISHERMAN

"El grande! El grande!" The guide was screaming, pointing at the fish twisting and wriggling at the end of Russell Jensen's line. A native of the Wai Wai tribe, the Amazon boatman was ecstatic, almost ready to break into a dance. Fisherman and guide stood beside the Rio Jatapu, a dark, winding waterway deep in the Amazon rain forest. Lined with lush green, the waterway twists and wends its way between trundling hills and low-lying sandbars on its way to meet the larger Rio Uatuma, as if trying to lose itself in the dense jungle. In the canopy of trees beside the river, anacondas and jaguars were settling in to sleep away the new day.

A retired contractor who spent most of his career working as a general foreman for New York University, Russell Jensen traveled four thousand miles from the Bronx to hear his guide utter just these words—"the Big One." He'd come in search of black piranha,

Russell Jensen has made a science out of landing big fish, breaking more than twen-ty world records. To catch the biggest black piranha ever taken, the Bronx resident traveled all the way to the deep, dark Amazon, pulling this toothy, eight-pound–four-ounce piranha out of the Rio Jatapu in 2009.
COURTESY OF THE IGFA

fabled man-eaters that attack aggressively, stripping everything they find down to the bone.

Of the many species of these misunderstood monsters, the black piranha (*Serrasalmus rhombeus*)—sometimes called the red-eyed piranha—is among the largest. The previous world record for the fish was seven pounds six ounces, and Russell Jensen meant to break it. And there is no place better in the world to find the black piranha than at the northern edge of the world's largest watershed—the great Amazon Basin.

Jensen and his guide had started their day at 6:30 a.m.—this was the New Yorker's last day of fishing before he had to leave for the long journey north—walking down to the Jatapu to fish for bait. Once they had buckets full, they'd push on in search of a world-beater. The Big One.

"El grande! El grande!"

The guide was, as Jensen puts it, "freaking out." He knew these waters, knew that you should never swim between 6 and 10 a.m. when the piranhas were feeding, knew the grey fighters live in both churning whitewater and deeper slow currents, and he was pointing at the fish shimmying on the hook, barely able to contain himself with excitement.

Jensen, not so much. An experienced angler, the New Yorker also knew his fish—specifically, what a trophy looks like. At his home in the Bronx, he has a room full of them, caught on excursions just like this one—to Alaska in search of king salmon, to Mexico on the trail of yellowfin tuna, and to Costa Rica to fish for tarpon. He's had a remarkable success rate.

Jensen had been to the Amazon five years earlier, fishing for jau, the largest of the two hundred species of catfish, with the same outfitter, Acute Angling of New Jersey. He spent six days on that trip before he landed a 109-pound whopper that broke the world record.

Only a few other fishermen across the globe could claim to be more successful than Russell Jensen. Bearing a resemblance to Ernest Borgnine, he's earned himself more than twenty world records. He'd wrestled lingcod from Alaska and hauled Orinoco peacock bass from Brazil. He'd taken a good-size black piranha already on this six-day excursion, a seven-pounder, but he wanted a bigger one. "I knew there were piranha over eight pounds in these waters," he says. "This fish wasn't big enough to hold the record a long time."

And this wasn't what a world beater looked like.

But there was his guide jumping up and down at the river's edge, shouting "El grande," "El grande mandi" and carrying on, gesturing with astonishment at this leviathan from the deep. On the hook was a fish that looked to Jensen like baitfish *bait*. A tiny thing, it couldn't have been more than a pound or two.

"I said, 'it's so cute,'" Jensen recalls. His guide, fully aware of the size this species usually reaches, insisted Jensen measure and weigh the little fellow. He did, and the rest was, well, stuff for the history books. Though it clocked out at a weighty two pounds four ounces, the pescadito was indeed "grande," the largest mandi catfish ever to be landed.

Russell Jensen had broken another world record. This time, without even trying.

●

This wasn't the way it normally happened for Russell Jensen. Each of the records that he'd beaten previously had been the result of painstaking planning, research, and practice—along with a certain amount of confidence. He liked to tell people, "I'm going to catch a world-record catfish or piranha" long before he ever dropped a line for one.

His inspiration came from an unlikely source. "I watched Tiger Woods," he says, "and he said practice, practice, practice." So practice he did. He'd spend hours aiming lines into his sister's swimming pool in nearby Connecticut. Cast, reel, cast, repeat. "I wanted to be the best." He still practices at least ten hours every week. "Now, I can drop my lure within six inches of where I want to be at thirty feet."

But it doesn't matter if you can hit a target if you don't know where the fish will be. Jensen believes practice is no good without research. You have to think like a fish. Understand the fish. Know what the fish wants and when it wants it. Anticipate its moves.

Jensen hung around those who know such things. When he wasn't overseeing new construction or maintaining old construction at NYU, the fisherman visited the school's biology department. "I got to know the professors of ichthyology," he says. He'd pick their brains about fish habits and habitats, listening intently as they explained the finer points of fish biology.

Studying was key. Not only did he make the acquaintance of people who might help him, he also spent many hours in the library and in front of the computer screen. Whatever fish he was hunting, he'd spend countless hours reading about.

"If I wanted to go after catfish, for example, I'd find out which is bigger—male or female. It's the female. When does she lay her eggs? First week in February. Then I [make plans to] go the last week of January because she'll be ravenous, eating everything to be ready to sit on the eggs."

●

Russell Jensen discovered his fishing skills almost by accident. "My father gave me a fishing pole when I was nine and told me to go catch a fish," he recalls. So he did. The Bronx boy went to a pond at the local cemetery, sunk his line, and drew it out with a carp attached. He hurried home, excited to cook the small fish for dinner. His father asked him where he caught it, and when he heard it came from a graveyard pool, he told his son to throw it out. Jensen was crestfallen.

But the boy was hooked. Though his father was no fisherman, he had a friend who was. This friend had a son about Jensen's age, and he invited young Russell along on saltwater fishing trips out of Montauk, New York. It was all new and exciting to the kid from the Bronx, but he was as green as the sea.

"I remember standing with my rod bent at the railing and saying to the mate, 'My line is stuck,' he recalls. "And the mate says, 'No, you've caught a fifteen- or sixteen-pound codfish.' I probably weighed all of eighty pounds myself."

Jensen seemed a natural, and he was soon outfishing his father's friend. "He was second to me. I caught the biggest fish. He only took me one or two times . . ." Landing the day's best catch became a habit. "I was nine years old. The next time out, I won two pools." The adults were either embarrassed or annoyed by the kid, and they stopped inviting him. "No one would take me."

Jensen fished where and when he could after that, but he didn't get serious again until he went into the Army. Stationed at the 101st Airborne's base at Fort Campbell, Kentucky, he found some fishing buddies among his fellow paratroopers. They'd venture out on leave to Kentucky Lake, the largest man-made reservoir in the eastern United States, and spend weekends dropping lines for bass, perch, bluegills, and catfish.

One of his captains arranged a trip to Alaska, and the Last Frontier is where Russell Jensen first started thinking about world records. "I was supposed to fish with three other fishermen on a forty-five-foot boat for halibut and king salmon," he says. "But the three others were coming in a different plane, and they weren't able

Black piranha grow quite slowly. In captivity, they might live as long as twenty
ars. To reach record size, a fish would have to be quite old indeed.

to fly." Jensen had the boat all to himself. "I fished all week with the captain and the first mate."

On one particular morning, Jensen's life would change. The New Yorker had caught his limit by 8:30 a.m., and they couldn't go back until 2:30, so the captain said he'd show Jensen his favorite spot, a sandbar near Elephant Cove with breathtaking visibility at low tide. "It was eight feet deep, and you could see right to the bottom. You can look at the fish and decide which one you want." The angler got excited. "I had the International Game Fish Association (IGFA) book with me—if I could catch a lingcod over twenty-three pounds, I would have a world record."

Some of the fish certainly looked like contenders, swimming tantalizingly below. "The captain said, 'where's your fly rod?' I told him I didn't bring it." He couldn't fish without one and bring home the record. Jensen swore then and there he'd be back the next year, and he asked the captain to keep the place a secret. "Don't take anyone else there," the fisherman said to the captain. "And he didn't."

Back in the Bronx, Jensen made his plans for the following year, and he decided he ought to know a little more about fly fishing. He signed up for classes at the Joan Wulff School of Fly Fishing in upstate New York, and he wasn't shy about telling Joan Wulff what he was about. "She asked everyone why they were there, and I told her I was there to break world records."

He said the same thing to his boss, the president of NYU, at the yearly staff picnic. "I told him I was going up to Alaska to shatter the world record—a lingcod on a fly rod." It wouldn't be easy. "The record was twenty-four pounds, so to *shatter* it I'd have to catch a fish over thirty pounds on a fly-fishing line." He spent a lot of time casting into his sister's pool.

All of the research, the painstaking preparation, the hours of practice paid off. "I caught a thirty-six-pounder," he says. And upon feeling the rush of reeling in a world beater, Jensen decided he needed another—"I wanted to be the best, to have the most world records"—and he decided to get serious about it. "If you make up your mind in this great country we live in, you can do anything," he says.

He reeled in another and another and another: a jundia catfish pushing 26 pounds; a silver croaker weighing in at a hefty 11 pounds, 4 ounces; and the biggest big one, a piriaiba catfish weighing 295 pounds 9 ounces, capable of sinking a ship. The trophy room at his house filled quickly, and he rose up the ranks of record holders. By 2008, he was the third-best fisherman in the world. To be Number 1—the Tiger Woods of sportfishing—he'd need more records. Which led him far south once again, to the tropical rainforest of the Amazon.

●

It was a place Russell Jensen always wanted to go. "The jungle, the jaguar, the anaconda . . ." he trails off. As a boy he had daydreamed about adventures in the Amazon—and finally he was there. He traveled twenty miles downriver with his Wai Wai guide, moving slowly, searching for piranha, fishing all the while. The black piranha can grow to be a football-size fish, and has a powerful jaw set with a circle of serrated white teeth. They're among the world's most aggressive animal species, known to terrorize aquariums in captivity, and they'll often go after creatures much larger than themselves. Piranha have attacked people on many occasions. In 2011, for example, piranhas chewed up a Bolivian teen when he jumped out of his canoe, causing so much damage he bled to death.

Russell Jensen knew much better than to leap from his boat. As excited as he was about going after these vicious predators, he was just as intrigued by the wild country they inhabited. "I took a picture of the fer-de-lance, one of the most venomous snakes in the Amazon," he says. "They call it a four-step—if it bites you, you have four steps." After that he spotted an eighteen-foot anaconda, then a twenty-two-foot anaconda—and the fabled big cat. "I saw a jaguar on the branch of a tree—it was about fifty feet from me." The fishing and fauna were spectacular, but so were the other sights: the river itself, the jungle, the indigenous culture. "I have pictures of hieroglyphs on rocks over four thousand years old."

On his very last day, Jensen made the catch. He had his custom Grant rod, crafted to his specifications, loaded with Power Pro eighty-pound line. At the end was a rugged Gamakatsu Octopus circular hook. "With this rig, I can catch over nine hundred pounds," says the fisherman. "And what do I catch? An eight-pound–seven-ounce piranha."

But it was just the fish he was after.

El grande.

2

BLACK MARLIN

ALFRED GLASSELL, FISHERMAN

nd this is how the other half does it. The 1 percent. Alfred Glassell was interested in fishing. Alfred Glassell had resources: the kind of play money that comes from having a father who was among the vanguard of American oil men, the kind of wealth that allowed him to amass the largest collection of African gold in the world. Alfred Glassell decided to use his riches to commission a team of Yale marine biologists to find him the world's greatest fishing hole.

And they found it.

Alfred Glassell traveled to the spot discovered by his scientists, set up an exclusive, world-famous fishing club, and reeled in the biggest bony fish ever caught with rod and reel, a 1,560-pound black marlin.

Today, the fish is in the Smithsonian.

Texas oil man Alfred Glassell decided he wanted to find the world's finest fishing hole, so he hired a team of biologists to sail the seas, studying ocean currents and fish populations. He discovered the fertile fisheries of Cabo Blanco, on the coast of Peru, and set up a famous fishing club with a group of affluent anglers, attracting the likes of Ernest Hemingway, Jimmy Stewart, and Doris Day. That's where he caught this 1,560-*pound* black marlin in 1953. The massive billfish remains the biggest bony fish ever caught and resides today in the Smithsonian.
COURTESY OF THE IGFA

•

Alfred Glassell Jr.'s entire life was one for the books. He was born into a Louisiana oil family in 1913, just as the automobile was taking over the nation, and came up through the schools of Shreveport. At Louisiana State, he blossomed. He was student body president, won entrance to Kappa Alpha, was a member of thirteen honor societies, and was a commander in the ROTC.

Upon graduation, the young scion migrated to Texas and worked in the family business. This was during the boom times for oil, and Glassell's company opened vast fields in Texas, Louisiana, and the Gulf of Mexico. All that was needed was a way to ship the black gold to the hungry markets of the northeast. So Glassell set up the Transcontinental Gas Pipe Line Corporation, later known as Transco, which ran the first transmission line from Texas to New York. The oil flowed one way; the money flowed the other.

When war broke out in the forties, the Texan enlisted, becoming a major in the Army. His service took him to both North Africa and Europe, and he was honorably discharged.

Glassell picked up his fishing pole upon his return. He had a lifelong interest in the outdoors, no doubt fostered by his father, who was a conservationist and one of the founders of Ducks Unlimited. Alfred Glassell the younger had a particular fondness for the underwater world, perhaps begun at the tender age of three, when he landed a four-pound bass.

Growing up, Alfred Jr. fished the lakes and bayous of his home state and searched the Gulf Coast for larger trophies, but he didn't realize his love for big fish until he went on a trip to the Bahamas with a friend. There was a big run of tuna on at the time and Glassell and his buddy decided to try and land an albacore. In a 2008 interview with journalist C. J. Schexnayder for kleph.com, Glassell describes the experience: "One afternoon, for the lack of anything else to do, we went out. We hooked one of those big tuna and I told myself right then 'this is for me.'"

The experience thrilled him. "It's the most exciting thing in the world. You go from complete relaxation to the maximum speed of a human body in the space of a single second. There is nothing in the world as exciting. . . . It's like a freight train coming out of the water and jumping into the air and throwing its body around with these beautiful leaps then throwing its bill around and diving back into the water and creating this huge geyser of spray."

Glassell wanted more, and he began to take trips to Bimini to fish. He and several friends started a de facto club, and they'd get together annually to search the waters off the island for bigger and better fish. They fished with a famous writer named Ernest Hemingway. Glassell didn't know it then, but he'd cross paths with the larger-than-life scribe in a meaningful way in a few years.

While on these trips to the Bahamas' westernmost isle, Glassell encountered Michael Lerner, a well-known fisherman (and IGFA founder) who had a lab onboard his boat, the *Bahama Mama*. Lerner realized the more that he knew about fish, the better he would be at catching them. (And he was very good: *Life* magazine once wrote that Lerner caught more big ones than anyone alive.) This seemed to make an impression on Glassell. "I'd give 'em my fish so he could put the scientifics to 'em," he told Schexnayder.

Lerner, one of the world's great anglers, worked with biologists to study fish populations—today there's a research station named for him in his beloved Bimini—and Glassell decided he'd lend his vast resources to the cause. In the late 1940s, he commissioned a Yale-Miami study of the relationship between sea currents and sea life. He funded the research vessel *Argosy*, a 110-foot steel ketch, which took teams of scientists from Yale and Miami all around the globe in a search for life. One year, the ship traveled more than twenty-four thousand miles. "We kept constant studies going on over the oceans of the world," Glassell told Schexnayder, "and we were particularly interested in concentrations of plankton. When you found an abundance of plankton you would find the fish, and we found a spot off the west coast of South America with a huge concentration."

It was a find that would change his life.

•

The place was called Cabo Blanco, and it sat four degrees south of the equator on the westernmost point of South America, at the great curve of the continent, the elbow of Peru that juts out into the Pacific. This is where the two prevailing currents of the world's largest ocean met in a swirling mass of life. As the *Miami News* put it: "Just off Cabo Blanco, the Humboldt and Equatorial Currents join, creating an ichthyological traffic jam—an unprecedented abundance and variety of fish, large and small, like nothing found anywhere else in the world."

This confluence—and the rich habitat it created—was exactly the fishing hole that Alfred Glassell was looking for. Reports of giant schools and huge tuna started filtering back to the oil man. A friend with a tuna fishing boat offered to take the eager angler south, and the pair visited Cabo Blanco at the dawn of the 1950s. Glassell was smitten. "Oh boy," he told Schexnayder, "it was the Mecca, the Heaven, the Valhalla of all fishing." Cabo Blanco was a tiny, remote outpost at what seemed the end of the earth. Staring at the sea from atop brown cliffs and dotted with white beaches, the village was very difficult to get to, requiring a nine-hour flight from Miami and then an arduous overland trek from the airport in Talara. None of that mattered to Glassell. Upon returning to the United States, he told his friend Kip Farrington, another wealthy fisherman who'd made a name for himself in the tropics, about the almost mythical charms of the White Cape, and they set about recruiting other interested parties for another big fish club. They had no trouble finding game fishermen and soon had a group of ten ready to invest in a clubhouse there. It was May of 1951.

And the Cabo Blanco Fishing Club was born.

The club was as exclusive as they come. Membership was limited to twenty and said to be in the ten-thousand-dollar range. Legend has it that Farrington was hounded by aspiring anglers, once turning down an offer of fifty thousand dollars to join. The ranks were mostly Americans—the likes of Firestone heir Roger Firestone, Buffalo Sabres owner Northrup Knox, Los Angeles tax attorney Joseph Peeler, ballistics baron John M. Olin, and Indianapolis Speedway magnate Anton Hulman—but included nabobs like Peruvian banker Enriquo Pardo Heeren as well. The fishermen rarely visited at the same time. Glassell himself made it a point to spend at least ten days at Cabo Blanco every year, usually in August. Members were allowed to have guests, and visitors would pay twenty-five dollars per person for room and board and one hundred dollars more to use one of the club's three boats, one forty-foot and two thirty-eight-foot vessels. Like Glassell's own *Miss Texas*, with its open back, fighting chair, and cabin, these were down-east-style craft imported from Nova Scotia.

The clubhouse was a simple, whitewashed structure, sitting atop a three-hundred-foot cliff overlooking the sea. With ten rooms, its own bar, pool, and cooking and cleaning staff, it was quite comfortable without being extravagant. These men were here to fish.

Fish they did. The billfish were so plentiful on "Black Marlin Boulevard," as the waters offshore were nicknamed, that members could simply cast in their direction and be fairly assured they'd take one home. They took so many they lined the driveway down to the dock—where a big crane sat at the ready to hoist fish—with marlin tails by the dozen. And they sent scores back to Miami to be mounted by renowned taxidermist Al Pflueger.

Alfred Glassell, though, took the first big one. On April 4, 1952, he landed what would become a world first—a bony fish over 1,000 pounds taken on rod and reel. (Glassell vied for that honor with Western writer Zane Grey, who caught a Giant Tahitian striped marlin that weighed a cool 1,040 pounds in 1931. That fish, however, was considered too shark-eaten to count.) The Texan's massive billfish

Modern methods for catching marlin include using multiple rods with outriggers to troll through likely water. The equipment and methods available to modern fishermen far outstrip what was available sixty years ago, making Glassell's accomplishment all the more impressive.

leaped from the briny up onto the clubhouse wall, and it would be the first of many "granders" at Cabo Blanco.

The record wouldn't last long. The waters were so rife with marlin here that a new record would be broken before the ink could dry on the previous one. Thousand-pounders became commonplace. "After the club was running people were catching them pretty often," Glassell told Schexnayder. "A total of thirty-two granders were caught there."

•

None would be bigger than this one. The catch came on a sunny early August day in 1953. Glassell was fishing about eight miles out, a five-pound mackerel on the end of his hook, when he felt a sharp jab on his line. His rod was a bamboo seven-footer, his reel a Fin-Nor, and his line thirty-pound linen. He set the hook, and found himself involved in a tug of war with a fish the size of a Model T. The battle was pitched, and it was exhausting. The fish leaped over and over in desperation, trying to make its escape.

Black marlin are tenacious fighters, and some mariners consider them the fastest fish in the sea, hitting speeds of more than seventy miles an hour. They've been seen to stun their prey with a swipe of their long bills, which can reach upwards of four feet in length, and use it like a rapier to pierce other fish. Their fearsome swords inspired fear in early fishermen, and they've been known to spear human vessels—or simply launch themselves on deck and wreak havoc (like one that terrorized an Australian fishing boat in October of 2012).

Glassell found himself in quite a melee. "He didn't fight any harder than other fish, it was just stronger and longer," he told Schexnayder. Fish and fisherman dueled for almost two and a half hours. By this point, Glassell had already captured four granders himself, so he had a sense of what he was getting into.

His crew carefully kept the boat out of the way of the fish while the Texan wrestled the rod. Eventually the noble beast wore itself out with all its jumping, and Glassell was finally able to get the upper hand. When they finally got it onboard, he and his companions were astonished by the sheer enormity of the thing. "We had him in the boat," Glassell remembered, "and his girth was way bigger than anything that had ever been reported. I said, 'back to the dock, boys.'"

The giant black marlin was actually a her, and she was indeed a specimen—1,560 pounds, fourteen feet seven inches—taking the world record not only for the species but for all bony fish. It topped the previous champion—a marlin caught by Zane Grey's captain Laurie Mitchell—by a cool quarter ton. And it remains the biggest vertebrate fish—as opposed to cartilaginous shark—ever caught by a rod-and-reel angler. A longtime patron of both the arts and conservation, Glassell donated his trophy to the Smithsonian, where it can be found today.

The catch made Glassell something of a celebrity, the real live incarnation of Hemingway's Santiago. Magazines profiled him. "The Oilman and the Sea," read one headline. Hollywood looked him up when director John Sturges was making the 1958 film of Hemingway's *Old Man and the Sea*. *Sports Illustrated* put him on its cover in March of 1956.

Alfred Glassell, who already moved in socially prominent circles, soon found himself hobnobbing with the most famous of the famous. Hemingway himself made a guest appearance at the Cabo Blanco Fishing Club when the Spencer Tracy movie of his book was being shot. The manly writer spent almost six months there, and he impressed the world-record holder: "He was a damned good fisherman. He got up early and stayed out late and would work at it all day long."

Hemingway confirms this in one of the few writings he did of his time at Cabo Blanco: "We fished 32 days, from early morning until it was too rough to photograph and the seas ran like onrushing hills with snow blowing off the tops."

Papa's efforts resulted in a host of big fish, the most notable of which was a 910-pound marlin. He celebrated the way he celebrated most things—with a drink.

"Hemingway did a lot of drinking. He was a big drinker," Glassell recalled. "That's one of the reasons we were glad to get him to go down to the club. His bar bill kept us operating for a year."

Baseball great—and avid fisherman—Ted Williams was another visitor in December of 1954. He caught a 1,235-pound black marlin that vaulted him onto the club's wall of fame. Other famed figures to venture to Cabo Blanco included New York Governor Nelson Rockefeller, Jimmy Stewart, John Wayne, Paul Newman, Humphrey Bogart, Doris Day, and Marilyn Monroe. The reputation of Alfred Glassell's little guild of game fishermen spread worldwide.

•

But tides change. The Cabo Blanco Fishing Club enjoyed fifteen good years before new currents—both oceanic and political—brought an end to an era. Glassell described the sad situation to C. J. Schexnayder. "They had a revolution in Peru and we weren't allowed to even go there anymore. The people in charge decided they were going to make it a playground for their top political players so they could use the boats and use the club. They didn't really take care of the boats and eventually the boats all sank. So now the *Miss Texas* is out there somewhere at the bottom of the ocean."

Not only did the rule of Juan Velasco Alvarado dampen the ability of Americans to travel to Peru, but the fishing itself started to wane. Some biologists suspected that overfishing of anchovies—a black marlin staple—had something to do with it. Others assumed that the fish simply rode away on the undertow that brought them there in the first place.

Alfred Glassell would have had to stop fishing in 1986 anyway. Open-heart surgery put an end to his big-game hunts, and he turned his attention to his other great love—art. He'd always been heavily involved with the Museum of Fine Arts in Houston, but now he had even more time to devote to it. Today, the Glassell School of Art is named in his honor.

The maritime legacy of this Oilman of the Sea will always be remembered. His contributions to undersea research were recognized in 1971 when he was presented with the International Oceanographic Foundation Marine Science Award. Thirty years later, IGFA inducted him into its Hall of Fame.

And fifty years on, no angler has ever reeled in anything bigger.

3

STRIPED BASS

GREG MYERSON, FISHERMAN

Who knew all the good that could come from a crack vial? Connecticut fisherman Greg Myerson found a way to repurpose the glass ampules that dealers used to sell their rock—and it made him a world champion. "I was working as an apprentice—a lot of my family are union electricians—in the worst part of New Haven, and it was during the crack epidemic," he recalls. "I started drilling out sinkers, and I'd put bearings in crack vials and put them in the sinkers. It mimics the sound of a lobster crawling along the bottom."

Turns out striped bass like crack vials just as much as crackheads.

Myerson did a lot of experimenting to make sure he got just the right sound. He had a two-hundred-gallon aquarium at his home in Branford, and he'd use a stethoscope to listen to the clicks that crayfish make skittering along the bottom. "I messed around with different sizes of ball bearings until I got a sound that was close," he

A lifelong striped-bass fisherman, Greg Myerson invented a new lure that proved an amazing attraction to the popular species and won a prestigious 2011 tournament—and a world record—as a result. He followed up his record-making eighty-three-pounder with the globe's record catch-and-release striper in 2012.
COURTESY OF THE IGFA

says. "The biggest fish all hunt through sound and vibration, then their sense of smell. They use their eyes for the final attack."

The inventive angler soon found he was on to something. The "Rattle Sinker" worked. He used his creation during the 2010 On the Water Striper Cup, a massive bass tournament that stretches from Maine to New Jersey. "I didn't set out to win," he says. "I just wanted to catch some bass." Did he ever. His lure was like crack to a junkie, and he caught three 60-pound fish with it—the largest 68.75 pounds. It was good enough to take home the trophy. "I won Angler of the Year," he remembers, "but I had no idea what a big deal it was."

Myerson was invited to the On the Water awards dinner and decided to attend, again not really comprehending what it was all about. He was shocked by the size of the occasion. "There were thousands of people there," he says with a chuckle, "and I had to get up on stage." He took it all with aplomb. Not long after the event, he got a phone call from Tony Checko, author of *The Striped Bass 60+ Pound Club*, a book chronicling the world's best striper fishermen. "He said, 'No one's ever caught three sixties in a year before. You'll be more famous than Al McReynolds.' I didn't even know who Al McReynolds was."

He'd learn soon enough.

•

Albert McReynolds, of course, was the striped-bass world-record holder. A native of New Jersey, he knew Sinatra and Sammy Davis Jr. as a kid, and he was always drawn to the sea. He caught a 78.5-pounder fishing off the Vermont Avenue jetty in Atlantic City in September of 1982, using a Penn 710 reel loaded with green Ande twenty-pound line, and a five-and-a-half-inch blackback silver Rebel plug. And he became something of a celebrity over the course of thirty years, winning endorsements, making appearances, and attracting attention nationwide. Much of it unwanted. McReynolds was accused of cheating, was sued for money he made from tackle companies, and even had a guy pull a gun on him. He told writer Jim Hannon that if he knew what was coming, he'd have cut the line. "I didn't catch the devil that night," he famously said, "the devil caught me."

The striped bass—also known as striper, linesider, rockfish, pimpfish—is one of the prized trophies of sportfishing. The sleek, silver member of the Moronidae family is so popular it's the state fish of Maryland, Rhode Island, and South Carolina, and the saltwater state fish of New Hampshire, New York, New Jersey, and Virginia. They range from the St. Lawrence to Louisiana, swimming up rivers to spawn in freshwater but living their lives in the briny. Stripers can grow huge, reaching as much as six and a half feet, eating mostly small fish, crustaceans, small invertebrates, and squid. The largest ever recorded—caught in a net—weighed in at a monstrous 125 pounds.

Diners everywhere love the slightly sweet flavor of stripers, and they've been a staple of commercial fisherman along the East Coast for centuries. Like so many other fish, though, their great popularity led to a dangerous decline in their numbers. Overfishing almost led to their demise in the eighties—fewer than five million stripers remained—but they've since rebounded. Estimates now have their stocks back up closer to sixty million.

Greg Myerson caught a fifty-five-pound striped bass when he was a boy, and from that moment on he was in love. Even as a toddler he showed an aptitude for fishing, and he was always angling for new ways to, well, angle. "My mother said when I was two years old I fished in the sewer in front of my house. She always said it was a natural thing for me."

His parents were from Brooklyn, but they moved to Connecticut when he was two. The open spaces around their home in Branford were idyllic stomping grounds for young Greg. "I grew up around field and farms," he says. He always enjoyed both fishing

Stripers can be fished from a boat, as Myerson did when he caught his world record, as well as from shore. Tournaments and enthusiasts often make a distinction between boat-caught and shore-caught fish.

and hunting, and still bow hunts for deer ("hunting with a gun is too easy") and spent a great deal of his childhood in pursuit of fin or fur or feather. But fishing was always a particular favorite.

"Growing up I fished every day—bluegills, trout, saltwater, fresh water. When I was eleven or twelve a friend took me out striped-bass fishing. I loved it. That was it for me." The Myerson family home was not far from Long Island Sound, and young Greg desperately wanted his own boat. He devised a scheme to trap muskrats to earn some cash. "I made good money, too," he says. "People used to pay for furs, and I got pretty good at it." By the time he was thirteen he had his first boat—a seventeen-foot Brockway with a 1968 Evinrude, which he kept at Pier 69 Marina in North Branford. "I caught my first fifty-pounder with that boat."

Myerson's father had been diagnosed with Parkinson's the year prior, and the young Greg used his boat as a means to get on the water and clear his head. He'd ride his bike to the docks, grab his fishing gear, and shove off in search of stripers. Sometimes these odysseys would take him far out into Long Island Sound.

"I'd take that boat for twenty-mile trips at thirteen years old." he says. "No one asked where we were. It was just, 'be home at whatever hour.' I'd go out to the race, where the sound meets the Atlantic. I didn't have instruments. No lights." The little skipper found himself in trouble on a few occasions. "Party boats couldn't see me. They called the Coast Guard on me once, who called my parents. I had to stay local for a little bit after that."

He fished all the time. When he wasn't doing that, he was tying flies. "I trout fished and fly fished all through high school," he says. He also played football. A lot of football. A defensive end at Lyman Hall High School, Myerson was an all-state selection in 1985. And the collegiate scouts came calling.

"I had twenty or twenty-five free rides—full scholarships to Division-One schools," he says. There were a lot of offers to weigh, a lot of things to ponder. Like other scholarship players, Myerson was thinking about his chances of playing first-team ball, of playing in a winning program, of a future in the game after school. But for this particular defensive end, there was one college prerequisite more requisite than others—and it didn't have anything to do with the gridiron. Whatever institution of higher learning Greg Myerson selected would need to be on the water. "I chose the University of Rhode Island," he says, "so I could bass fish."

Myerson got a place in Point Judith, a small village in southern Rhode Island, staring out at Narragansett Bay. "It was right on the water, and I kept getting different boats, all pieces of junk. But I fished all the time with my buddies." When he wasn't playing linebacker.

After school he returned to his hometown and took a job as a union electrician. Which put him in that nasty New Haven neighborhood filled with crackheads—and spent vials. He spent time tinkering with his sinker idea until he found a sound that he thought worked. The "Rattle Sinker" was tested over and over again. And then he won the 2010 Striper Cup.

In 2011, he registered for the cup again, and again he pulled in another striped bass over sixty pounds. Another fifty-seven-pounder gave him a good shot at repeating as champion. But he had some competition. "I needed a fifty- or sixty-pound fish to win the tournament," he recalls, "and that's when I caught the world record."

•

It was the perfect night. At least that's what Myerson told his friend, Matt Farina, as they loaded up Myerson's skiff and pulled out into the Sound. "He just started fishing and he wanted to go every night," Myerson says. But on this particular evening—August 4— the conditions were just as the angler wanted them. A night for catching big fish.

"I always look for what I figure are the best days," Myerson explains. "A slack high tide around sunset on a first quarter moon. Fish frenzy around then, and those are my prime times," he says. The pair motored the boat out toward the footballer's favorite spot on Six Mile Reef.

"I fish where the lobster are," he says. "There are always a lot of bass where the lobster are. They like lobster, and big bass are lazy. Around slack tide the lobsters come out to feed." On his way out to the reef he paused near a favorite rock. "It's a big boulder where there's always a lot of lobster fishing." Myerson attached a Rattle Sinker to his six-and-a-half-foot St. Croix tuna rod. It sported a Quantum Cabo reel loaded with fifty-pound Berkley Gorilla Braid. Over the side it went and Myerson let it fall down to the bottom. The two friends quieted down. The fisherman believes one of the secrets to fishing success is stealth. Surface noise disturbs the fish and they won't bite.

Whatever they were doing, it worked.

"I felt the fish hit, and I went to set the hook. I had a big eel on. I missed." The big bass came back again and made another grab. This time it took. "I set the hook on her, and the fish didn't budge. She inhaled the eel, and I set the hook. She shook her head a few times. The rod was just jacked up." Once hooked, the fish began to swim, pulling almost sixty feet of line off the reel in seconds. The boat started to follow behind her. "She towed us for about twenty minutes."

The moon was shining brightly off the surface of the sound. Suddenly, the fish jumped as only the big bass can. "She porpoised out, water flew twelve feet in all directions, and I could see her dorsal fin. It was the biggest one I'd ever seen." Myerson and the bass did battle for twenty minutes before it lay quiet on the bottom. Then the angler began to pull line in. When he got it to the side of the boat he was astonished. "I couldn't believe how big it was."

Farina went to net the fish, but "he wasn't the most experienced and the net got caught on the swimming platform," remembers Myerson. The pair started to panic. "I was barefoot, and I slipped as we were pulling it in." Myerson slammed into a gunwale so hard he'd have to go see a doctor the following day—the linebacker thought he'd broken his ribs. He jumped to his feet, and he and Farina scrambled about, afraid they were going to lose the fish. "The whole net handle started to bend," the angler recalls. "I grabbed the net straight up and just hauled on it."

After much wrestling, the giant sea bass was in the boat. Myerson was in a state of awe. "I really didn't want to keep it because the fish was beautiful. I knew it was going to make me win the tournament."

He and Farina put the fish in the hold and went out for more—it was too fine an evening to head back. "We fished all night and caught a dozen more fish, but we only kept this one." Every half hour or so Myerson would walk to the hold and peer in at his fish, not quite believing how big it was.

They returned to the dock and showed the champion striper to others who were there. Drinks started flowing, and the angler did a bit of celebrating. He knew he'd won the tournament.

It was late when he got home. "Around midnight we pulled in and I said, "let's weigh this thing."" Myerson and Farina hooked the fish onto a scale the angler had on his garage. They both had ideas about where the needle would stop but neither was quite prepared for what the scale read: "It said eighty-three pounds," Myerson says. "I said, 'that can't be right.'"

In the morning he drove the fish over to Jack's Shoreline Bait and Tackle in Westbrook. "When I got there, there were probably fifty guys waiting. They all knew it was a world record."

It might easily have been somebody else's. "The fish had a line in its mouth," Myerson says. "And it had a treble hook in the side of its mouth. Two people had already caught that fish."

●

Catch a trophy fish—especially if it's the world record of the most coveted saltwater species—and people are going to want to know the whats and wheres. "People are always asking what I caught it with," Myerson says, and he has the perfect answer.

When the inventive fisherman first explained his theories behind the Rattle Sinker, people would often exclaim: "'Dude, why don't you patent that thing?"

Patent's pending.

Myerson took his little rig to the University of Connecticut's Law School, and students there helped him with the patent paperwork gratis. And he's put his Rattle Sinker up for sale at Guide's Choice Tackle on Staten Island.

"A lot of people who have bought it have started to catch big bass." He says. "To turn a big fish's head you need something a little extra. I'll never fish without it."

No high-pressure sales needed. Myerson only has to tell prospective buyers that he's caught *two* world records with it.

Wait, two?

"Yeah, I set the record for catch-and-release striped bass."

This was a 3.7-foot striper that Myerson caught in May 2012. The IGFA created the new category as a no-kill alternative to its all-tackle records (see the Afterword), and it doesn't have a weight requirement, relying solely on length. But the fisherman estimates the 3.7-foot bass weighed fifty pounds or more.

Not bad for a little crack vial.

4

WALLEYE
MABRY HARPER, FISHERMAN

At first glance it seems a rather ordinary snapshot. A man stares out of a gritty black-and-white image with the barest hint of a smile on his face. Cracked around the edges with age, the picture shows a fisherman in tall grass, hardwoods towering over him in the background. Thin and wiry, he's wearing a T-shirt, and a cap is shading his face. Words are scrawled in cursive across the sky, but they're hard to make out. It's a timeless shot, the sort of photograph that could have fallen out of anyone's family album—it actually came from one—nothing exceptional about it.

Except for the fish.

The lucky angler, arms bent at the elbow, hands about shoulder length apart, is holding a massive walleye, gripping its tail and gills. With its mouth wide open and the sort of face only a fisherman could love, the forty-one-inch prize is so large the man is leaning

This old photograph of Tennessee angler Mabry Harper posing with his 25.4-pound, forty-one-inch, world-record walleye caused an uproar in 1996 when *Outdoor Life* challenged his 1960 catch.
COURTESY OF THE HARPER FAMILY AND JOHN OLIVER

over slightly and his elbows are resting on his belt to help support its weight. No question it's a trophy.

The photo doesn't show the man—a Tennessean named Mabry Harper—doing anything unusual. He isn't pictured doing anything untoward with the fish. There's no secret lover in the background, or bag of stolen cash, or communist flag. It's just a simple photograph of a man with a fish.

Amazing the ruckus a simple picture of a man with a fish can cause.

•

The year was 1960 and Mabry Harper was spending an August night doing what he loved—fishing. A plumber and steamfitter by trade, employed at Tennessee Tech, a university in Cookeville, he'd gone to Old Hickory Lake on the first of the month looking to land some catfish. The lake had only been created six years prior, when the Old Hickory Lock and Dam were built, holding back the flow of the Cumberland River, twenty-five miles northeast of Nashville. Named for "Old Hickory" himself, President Andrew Jackson, who lived nearby, it's a wide, winding waterway, lined with greenery, coiled like a sleeping snake in north central Tennessee.

Harper grew up in Hartsville and often spent weekends on the river. Now fifty-six, a father with a five-year-old son and a stepson, he lived in Cookeville, about an hour away, and he often stayed with family in town and then took off fishing. His favored spot was about nine miles upriver from the Second Creek Boat Dock—the county's only access onto the Cumberland—at a place near a farm owned by the Sanford family.

A veteran on the angle, he readied his rod. It was strung with seventy-five-pound monofilament test line and had a star drag reel. He put a silverback on his #6/0 hook, and cast out into a section of the river shaded by a large limestone bluff.

Eventually a fish was interested, only it wasn't a catfish, but rather a walleye, the long slender cousin of the perch. Harper would tell reporters later that it took his line "like a freight train." As Trousdale County historian John Oliver notes, the plumber was used to big fish. He'd caught a ninety-pound catfish not long before and that was what he thought was on the line now.

The fight took the better part of an hour—somewhere around fifty minutes. When it breached, Harper was surprised to see it was a walleye, or a "jack" as the locals called them. And it was a good-sized one. Harper figured it would make a tasty treat for his family, just like the seventeen- and nineteen-pound jacks he'd recently brought home.

"He caught the walleye but he wasn't too interested in it," John Oliver says. "He was fishing for catfish." His stepson Jerry and his nephew "Sheep" came by to bring him a brown paper bag full of breakfast that Mary had cooked up for him. They were struck by the big jack that Harper had dangling from the side of his boat, and they asked if they could take it in to weigh and measure it.

Most walleye grow to be one to five pounds—this one weighed considerably more than that. Jerry and Sheep hefted the fish into an old washtub in the back of Sheep's truck and took the fish to the dock, where there were both scales and a camera. Because this was the access point for the river, people often gathered here to fish off the dock and put in their various craft. It wasn't long before a crowd had gathered to gawk at the monster.

Spurred on by the crowd, Harper's stepson helped Mel Royster, the dock's owner, bring the fish over the scale. According to historian John Oliver, Royster quickly realized how immense this fish was, and he wasn't surprised to see the scale read twenty-five pounds four ounces—an astonishing size for this member of the perch family. If you caught a walleye of fourteen pounds, you thought you'd hit the big one. Anything bigger than that was considered a genetic anomaly, a freak. And, of course, a lucky landing—a fish that big made for a lot of tasty filets. Bob Miles, one of the workers at the dock, put a tape to the thing: forty-one inches. Truly a massive jack. Someone recommended they contact Jim Spurling, the game warden for Trousdale, Macon, Wilson, and Smith Counties, who lived right there in Hartsville.

Mary Harper arrived along with a host of others. Everyone was astonished by the size of this fish and stood around swapping stories.

Meanwhile, while all this hubbub was happening on shore, Mabry Harper was happily out in his boat on the river looking for a damned catfish this time. He remained out on the water until his stomach told him it was time for lunch. When he returned to the dock he was surprised to see his wife, friends and neighbors, and the game warden all waiting to talk to him. Spurling asked him a few questions and he answered them. Then he ate lunch and went back out to fish away the rest of the afternoon.

Harper took the walleye home, lopped off its head, and cut and cleaned it. Then Mary rolled it in cornmeal and seasonings and fried it on the stovetop. The family sat down to enjoy it for dinner.

The next day Jim Spurling got a call from Dr. Glenn Gentry, who was a biologist with the Tennessee Fish and Game Commission. Not only was Harper's fish a Tennessee record, it was a world record, handily besting the previous twenty-two-pound–four-ounce beast caught in Fort Erie, Ontario, in 1943. The warden drove to the farm where Harper was staying and told him the good news—and asked to see the fish. Harper told him all he had left was the head, which he'd saved to mount.

Harper was over the moon. He registered the fish with *Field & Stream* magazine, the Henry Holt-owned publication that kept official fishing records in the sixties. Then he did countless interviews with sportswriters from across the country, and his wife kept all the clippings she could get her hands on.

"Our dad loved fishing and was a really good fisherman," Harper's stepson Jerry Robertson said in an interview years later. "He took a lot of pride in having caught a world-record fish."

Newly released photos of Mabry Harper's fish, shown here with his wife, Mary were used to vindicate the plumber's catch.

Of course, records are meant to be broken—or at the very least challenged.

•

The murmurs and rumblings started decades ago. Many fishermen were skeptical when they read about Harper's catch in the record books—sounded too much like a fish story. Walleye simply didn't get that big. This was a species that was considered good-sized when it hit five pounds. To grow larger than twenty-five pounds it would need a perfect environment. Was an artificially created lake such a place?

The previous world record had been twenty-two pounds. State records in most cases were nowhere near that large. Connecticut's, for example, was fourteen and a half pounds. Michigan's a little over seventeen. Wisconsin's was eighteen. Mabry Harper must have been exaggerating—or he had padded his numbers somehow.

Another Tennessean was found to have done just that not long before Harper's catch. Well, sort of. D. L. Hayes landed what he called a world-record small-mouth in Dale Hollow Lake, one hundred miles northeast of Old Hickory, in 1955. It was just an ounce shy of nine pounds—but three of those pounds were from the lead weight the employee of a resort looking for publicity had packed inside. Likewise, the world-record muskie weighed sixty-nine pounds fifteen ounces—if you counted the sand in the fish's guts.

Naturally, fishermen suspected something was up with the walleye record, too. Harper's trophy fish was long gone—it was never mounted—so it didn't exist to examine further. Harper himself died a few years after his catch, so he couldn't defend himself. The only remaining hard evidence was in the photographs.

The challenges came in. Questions were asked. Famous fishermen like Al and Ron Lindner ran editorials in *In Fisherman* magazine expressing their doubts. Harper's catch just didn't add up. *In Fisherman*'s staff biologist Steve Quinn studied the situation. He's quoted as saying: "A 29-inch girth isn't physically possible for a walleye 41 inches long. Using a time-tested formula (girth2 x length ÷ 800), those measurements describe a fish weighing close to 40 pounds." And the magazine didn't think the setting and time of year seemed likely either, quoting an unnamed Arkansas fisheries biologist, who said, "I really doubt that a walleye could weigh 25 pounds in August. Maybe in February, but not in August."

And then in June of 1996 came the big one. *Outdoor Life* ran a story by a writer named Dick Sternberg that asserted that Mabry Harper's fish could not have been as big as the Tennessean claimed—and Harper's own photos proved it. Basing all of his evidence on the picture of Harper proudly holding his catch, Sternburg argued that there was no way the fish in the picture was forty-one inches long. "During my sixteen-year career as a fisheries biologist and overseer of the Minnesota record-fish program," Sternberg wrote, "I handled hundreds of big walleyes and became pretty proficient at visually judging weight. The first time I saw a picture of Mabry Harper holding up his 'world-record' walleye, I remember thinking: 'That fish *can't* weigh 25 pounds. I still don't buy the record, and neither should anyone else. Here's why.'"

Fishy photographic forensics ensued.

The average length of a man's hand, Sternberg wrote, was about 3⅓ to 3¾ inches. He gave Harper the benefit of the doubt and conjectured that, even if the plumber had hands much larger than that, say, 4 inches, and you used that as a guide to measure the fish, it could only have been 34.45 inches long at maximum. Looking at the distance between his right hand—at the gills—and his left hand—near the tail—it seemed impossible for the walleye to measure almost three and a half feet. The author estimated that Harper's hand spread was about 4.5 inches, which was bigger than even "a

Walleye can be a long-lived fish, surviving as long as twenty-nine years. But in the wild, it's rare to catch a fish older than five or six years. A fish over twenty inches and four pounds or so is a prize indeed.

defensive lineman." If the fish wasn't as long as the fisherman said it was, then it was unlikely to be as heavy.

The National Freshwater Fishing Hall of Fame in Hayward, Wisconsin, was swayed. Down came the picture in the Hall of Harper's catch. The Tennessean's fish was disavowed, and the world record went to the next walleye in line, Al Nelson's twenty-two-pound–eleven-ounce giant caught in Greer's Ferry, Arkansas, in 1982. The Hall's director at the time, Ted Dzialo, told a reporter from *In Fisherman*: "Our board of governors meeting decided to disqualify the record based on measurements of Harper's hands in relation to the length and depth of the fish. . . . Harper caught a nice fish, no question. But we feel it couldn't have weighed 25 pounds."

Mabry Harper's record held with the International Game Fish Association, and *Field & Stream* never made any noises about pulling it. But the disavowal of the Freshwater Fishing Hall of Fame cast a shadow over Mabry Harper and his prize. The Hall never said it in so many words, but what they were implying was that the Tennessee angler was a cheat. A fraud. No better than fishermen who were stuffing weight in their catches. Trying to get away with something.

Was the Mona Lisa smile on Harper's face in that famous photo really a smirk?

•

But Mabry Harper had his defenders, too. John Oliver is the official historian of Harper's home county, Trousdale. He wanted justice both for the Harper family and for his neighbors in the county's only town, Hartsville. "When I moved to Trousdale County, the story of Mabry Harper and his famous fish was one of the first things I heard," he says. "I was a school teacher and had Mabry Harper's son in one of my classes and he was very proud of his father's record," he says. Another student came up to him one day and said, "Mr. Oliver do you know that Mabry Harper's record isn't the real record any-more?" "We hadn't heard about it," Oliver explains. "It wasn't in any of the local papers."

Oliver tracked down the story. "I read the article and thought, this guy has got it all wrong." The historian set about on a very methodical quest, using the same photometrics that got Harper in trouble in the first place—only he had more photos. "New" snap-shots were found of that historic day by Old Hickory Lake. Oliver went to see the Harper family. "They had a box of old photos that clearly proved the record was legitimate," he says.

In all the excitement on that fateful day in 1960, a lot of pho-tos were shot. There's the one of Mabry holding the walleye arms extended, yes, but also the one of his wife, Mary, smiling proudly with it in front of a 1959 Plymouth Suburban. She's struggling to hold the hefty walleye, too, kneeling before the vehicle. The tail of the fish is in front of the wheel well and the head halfway across the driver's side door. Another photo shows her in a similar pose. And there was one even more important image.

"When I saw the photo of Mary Harper holding the monster walleye, I instantly knew I had the proof I needed," Oliver explained in a piece in *Outdoor Life*. "I had a professional photographer blow up the photo of Mary to scale [to show] the fish would measure the official length of 41 inches. Once the photo was done, I measured Mary Harper's height. I put her at 5 feet 6 inches, which was later confirmed by her son."

If the fish was as long as Harper claimed, it was likely as heavy. The record, after all, is based on the weight of a catch. The historian spent a year tracking down more information. "By the time I had completed my investigation, I had sixty-five pages of notes, photos, articles, and interviews," Oliver says. He personally delivered his findings to the Freshwater Fishing Hall of Fame.

"I swear, the director looked at me like, 'Why are you here?'" One of the board of directors had been very kind to him and welcomed him to the Hall. "I sat down with them and showed them all the materials and their faces just turned ashen, like 'We've made a big mistake.'"

The Hall then commissioned its own study to look into Oliver's research. "Our verification process was exhaustive and scrutinizing," says Emmett Brown Jr., the Hall's current executive director. "We stand behind this fish, as we do with all of our other records."

John Dettloff, the Hall's president, wrote an essay laying out the Hall's verification methods. First and foremost was a reconsideration of the primary picture. In meticulous fashion, Dettloff debunks the *Outdoor Life* article's conclusions.

"This is simply just another case of today's overstated expectations not matching yesterday's photographic reality," he writes. Dettloff notes that photographers these days typically stand closer to their subjects than they used to, and they often use wide-angle lenses, which alter the perception of the viewer and "commonly make fish appear larger than they really are." As viewers, we've gotten used to that.

Next, he contends that the "hand spread" method of measurement—using the size of a known object to estimate the size of an unknown in a photograph—is fraught with potential problems. Perspective is difficult to judge in snapshots. And who's to say how large the Tennessean's hands were? In the *Outdoor Life* story, Sternberg assumed that Harper's hands were between three and a half and four inches wide, but, writes Dettloff, that discounts the possibility that he had unusually large mitts.

"The fact is: hand width can have a considerable variance from one person to another and often without regard for a person's physical size," he argued. "Laborers and tradesmen who work with their hands often have thick, muscular hands as a result of their lifelong vocations. And Harper, who was a plumber by trade, was very likely one such person." In other words, Harper could easily have hands that stretched four and a half inches, which would have discounted Sternberg's whole argument. Too many variables to be conclusive.

Then there are the other pictures, including one showing the fish's head lying on a bed of newspaper, cellophane, and tinfoil positioned right next to a ruler (a ruler that, incidentally, had the Bible's Golden Rule printed on it). Because of shadows and the irregular cut of the head, it's difficult to get a measure of the head in full, but Dettloff estimated that the distance from the jaw to the posterior of the eye socket was about three and seven-eighths inches. Using other walleye as scale, this would make the head itself eleven inches and the body *at least* thirty-nine inches.

Most convincing of all, though, was the testimony of warden James Spurling. Spurling knew a twenty-five-pound walleye would be a state-record walleye, and he did his double-checking. He swore it in an affidavit. John Oliver found that document.

Dated August 11, 1960, it read:

> *I, James H. Spurling, do hereby certify that on August 3, 1960 I checked the scale on which Mr. Harper's Walleye was weighed. The scales used to weigh the fish were found to be four ounces too heavy. The fish originally weighed 25 pounds and four ounces on the scales used by the Second Creek Boat Resort. The scales at the Second Creek Boat Resort were checked against a certi- fied state-inspected set of scales at Reese's Food Market in Harts- ville, Tennessee. The scales were inspected in February, 1960, by a State Inspector. The adjusted weight of the Walleye caught by Mr. Harper is 25 pounds."*
>
> *Signed, transcribed, and sworn to by the Trousdale County Clerk.*

●

So there *was* something wrong with Harper's record. There had been a little confusion. Four ounces of confusion. But it was the fault of the scales and not Mabry Harper. And the fish still outweighed the world-record walleye by almost three pounds. The Hartsville plumber was vindicated.

"He was a real character," says John Oliver. "A hard drinker, and a hard man, but he lived to fish. His family had probably a hundred pictures of him with fish. He was always fishing."

In May of 2010 the Hall officially voted to reinstate Harper's walleye. And back up went the photo in the Hall.

Is that a smile on Mabry Harper's face?

5

WALKING CATFISH

PATRICK KEOUGH, FISHERMAN

Patrick Keough was fishing with his kids in the backyard of his Florida apartment when he hooked the fish. Weighing a little over two pounds, it was long and dark, with the whiskers of a catfish, but it was like no catfish he'd ever seen. It was covered in white spots and slathered in a slime that clung to its body. The Army recruiter wasn't sure what it was. A native of the Sunshine State, he'd been fishing his whole life, and he dropped a line in Delray Lake almost every night. He and his son and daughter typically reeled in brown bullheads, largemouth bass, or peacock bass—or whatever else might be swimming around in the canals of south Florida.

This was one odd-looking fish. "It fought like a catfish," Keough recalls, "but when I pulled it up I had no idea what it was." Curious, he filled a bucket with water, scooped the fish into it, and left the bucket on the back porch.

Then he went inside to do some research and see just what it was.

It wasn't long before the screams started.

While Keough was in the house describing the strange creature to a fish biologist, the crazy catfish attempted an escape. "While I was on the phone, my wife started screaming," the fisherman says with a laugh. "The fish had climbed out of the bucket, and was pulling itself along the floor. My wife wasn't having it."

A lot of fish species will wriggle and squirm and try to free themselves from captivity, but few will do so as adroitly as this fish.

"I had never heard of a catfish that could climb out of a bucket," Keough says.

He had now.

The specialist in exotic species at the Florida Non-Native Fisheries Laboratory in Boca Raton knew just what it was; a walking catfish. The species is more commonly found in the Congo and the wetlands of southeast Asia but had been spotted in southeast America as early as the sixties. Keough took the fish down to the lab, and the biologist confirmed it—and told the angler that this was a *big* one. Perhaps even world-record big.

Wouldn't Keough's kids find that cool?

•

It was never about the trophy for Patrick Keough. Sure he took the fish to IGFA to have it weighed and documented and paid the fee to submit it for consideration, but it wasn't about all that. This was something cool he could share with his kids. He kept the ego out of fishing, doing it because he loves the outdoors and wanted to share that enthusiasm, and it was something that that the career Army man, his son, and his daughter could all look forward to after long deployments and long days in the office.

"I was never looking to catch any world records," he says. "Everything I do is for recreation, but anything I could do to keep my kids interested I'd do." Keough took his son and daughter fishing as often as he could. As they grew up, perhaps remembering how much fun he had as a kid when his uncles took him.

"I grew up in St. Augustine, Florida, and my uncles took me a lot. I was a kid who always wanted to be outside. Even the job I took in the Army—I was an infantryman—was outside. We're the ones who are always in the woods or off somewhere."

Keough spent his childhood fishing and hunting and diving. He liked to go inshore fishing in the salt just as much as he liked to cast into freshwater. "Striped bass, smallmouth, largemouth, white bass, catfish . . . whatever, I love it all."

When his children were young, they'd catch some fish and submit the big ones to Florida's trophy program. "The kids have a bunch of certificates from that. It was fun and kept them engaged," he says. "And it's really played out—they both still like doing this stuff with me and they're eighteen and twenty now." His daughter is now a high school senior; his son is twenty and just returning from a tour in Afghanistan. Both still love to go out fishing.

•

Patrick Keough took his love of fishing with him when he was sent to the Middle East in 2002. "Hunters are going to hunt, fishermen are going to fish, it doesn't matter where in the world you put them," he says. A first sergeant in the infantry, he was in the vanguard when the United States moved against the Taliban. "My regiment—the 187th—were some of the first forces in Afghanistan, and then we were among the first forces in Iraq. It was, like, invade Afghanistan, come home for a while, and then go invade Iraq."

The walking catfish is an aquatic oddity—covered in mucus, it can pull itself along on dry land with its fins. Though the species is not native to the United States, typically found in southeast Asia and the Congo, the Army's Patrick Keough caught this world-record specimen—just under three pounds—in the canals of Florida.
COURTESY OF THE IGFA

The Floridian was inevitably drawn to water. He was initially stationed near the Baghdad airport at one of Saddam's palaces, and he was amazed at the extent of the dictator's power. Saddam had rerouted waterways in the city and built his opulent compound right around his own artificial watershed. "He had pushed a lot of water and had a nice flow into his palaces, and he even had a little fishing village in one." Just as they had at Saddam's other mansion's, the soldiers securing the facility found treasure inside: "We found a lot of fishing gear and everything," laughs Keough. "It put the idea in my head. I never thought I would be fishing in the Iraqi desert."

After their mission in Baghdad, Keough's unit was sent to hold an Army "R&R" station at a place near "Saddam Dam," the biggest impoundment in Iraq. Now known as Mosul Dam, the aging structure walls the Tigris outside Mosul, the second-largest city in Iraq and the capital of Nineveh Province. It was here that the infantryman started fishing again, and he discovered that Saddam had his people cowed even when it came to something as elemental as fishing.

Iraqi fishermen had to scavenge bait and fish with simple handlines. Though they loved to eat fish, they were hesitant about keeping what they caught. "People would fish," Keough said of the Iraqis, "but all fish were considered Saddam's. They could fish scummy waters, where they'd pull eels and things out, but the good fish were Saddam's."

In Iraq, these good fish were called "boonie fish." "Kind of like a mix between a redfish and a carp," says Keough. "You could catch them on anything—a couple of heavy spoons—anything that was flashy. The people would catch one and be ecstatic. They'd cook it and eat it right away."

Spoons, though, weren't what Keough had in mind. He would stare out at the Tigris, and think about the gear that he took for granted back home. A plain old rod and reel and some lures.

He also felt the urge to teach the Iraqi kids how to fish, just as he had his own children. In his free time, he began writing letters.

"I wrote to Pradco and Shakespeare and other companies, and they started sending me all this free stuff," he recalls. When he got the gear, he sought out the children who lived in the area. "I did some free kid fishing days, things like that," he says.

And the Iraqi people, many of whom were very suspicious of the Americans, took right to it. Keough showed them how to land fish with actual tackle as opposed to handlines. "You know the old adage, 'teach a man to fish?'" he says, "it was like that. I started giving people rods, and we made all kinds of inroads."

The gear that was donated to him, he in turn donated to the Iraqis who would become the guides for the American soldiers who were sent to the station for rest and relaxation. In a way, his generosity came full circle, helping bring relief to his weary comrades. "Give a guy a fishing pole—who's been in combat for a while—and it takes him away, at least for a day."

●

The walking catfish would feel right at home in some of the scummy waters Keough found in Iraq. The homely creature takes its name from the very behavior that terrified Candace Keough—it can travel comfortably on dry land. An air breather, the fish is content out of water, as long as it stays moist, and it navigates by propping itself up on its pectoral fins and propelling itself forward by wiggling its hindquarters—sort of like an Army infantryman moving forward on hands and knees.

The fish evolved this way because of its habitat—stagnant pools, fetid swamps, rice paddies, flooded ditches, and other wetlands that eventually dry up. When the water drains off or evaporates, the itinerant beasts simply crawl their way to another basin, a coating of a mucuslike substance keeping them hydrated until they arrive.

Couple their slime with their long antennae- like barbels—and you have a fish that's plenty ugly. Typically about a foot long, walking catfish are gray or brown, covered in white spots, and have a few pairs of the sensors that allow them to feel their way around murky pools. Stingers behind their fins make them difficult to handle.

They're most commonly found just below the surface in places like the Mekong and Chao Phraya Rivers in Vietnam and Thailand and other shallow, swampy watersheds in Indonesia, Singapore, India, Bangladesh, Burma, and Brunei. The fish like fairly warm waters and live off smaller fish, mollusks, and aquatic weeds.

They're exotic—and unusual—enough that they occasionally land in the aquariums of fish collectors. And then they get dumped like the proverbial alligator in the toilet. Considered an invasive species in the United States, walking catfish have been spotted from Massachusetts to California and were first reported in Florida in 1967. Like so many other unusual species, they made their way to the Everglades, and eventually migrated into the Sunshine State's famous canals. Florida has more nonnative species than any other state, more than 439 animals, according to a recent study. These range from the famous pythons of the Everglades to Cuban tree frogs to Nile monitor lizards.

And everything seems to flush into the canals. One of these fed into Delray Lake, where Patrick Keough found himself in 1989. That was the year he was sent on a recruiting tour. He was going to be the smiling face of the US Army, the salesman who attracted new soldiers to a life in the military. And he hated it. "I didn't like recruiting," he says. "It wasn't my thing. I was stuck in an office for three years, and I'm an infantryman. I'd much rather be outdoors."

This particular tour of duty took him to Delray Beach, Florida, a city of sixty thousand in Palm Beach County known for its two-mile-long public beach and its tennis tournaments. Parallel to the waterfront is the Florida East Coast Canal, and along the canals sits Delray Lake, a man-made basin created when Interstate 95 was constructed. Keough and his family found an apartment right on the reservoir.

When he got home from work in the evening, Keough used to like to gather up his kids and head out back to throw a line in the lake. It was a way to both bond and relax after a day at the office. They'd catch peacock bass—"my kids and I have worn those peacock bass out"—as well as brown bullheads—"the kids loved fighting them"—and occasionally something unusual that had found its way into the canal system.

That's where he was on the night of May 30, 2001. His son had just hooked a bullhead, and Keough had cast in himself. He felt something take a bite, he set the hook, and he reeled in the freak fish. Onto the back porch it went into the fateful bucket, and inside he went to look it up online. Luckily, his surfing brought him to the Florida Non-Native Fisheries Laboratory. "Otherwise," he jokes, "I wouldn't have a world record for a fish nobody's ever heard of, which was probably thrown out of somebody's tank."

The fish was just under two pounds, which the biologist thought was quite large. "It's funny," Keough says, "I go online to look up the record and find out that IGFA is in Dania Beach, Florida, about a half hour down the road." The recruiter took his fish to be weighed and measured and discovered that, yes indeed, it was world-record size.

He had caught the largest walking catfish ever recorded—in a place where there are hardly any catfish walking.

He sent in his paperwork. There was no fanfare, no instant celebrity status, no sponsors calling to endorse him, no news cameras lining up outside to interview him. This was a world record the world ignored. He got a certificate in the mail, just like his kids had before him.

And Patrick Keough, his son, and his daughter kept on fishing. A couple of months later, on July 7, 2001, he was at it again in the backyard with his son, using a Berkeley Lightning Rod, with an Abu Garcia MX130R reel, and twelve-pound Berkley line. And they were joking about the catfish. "My son was pulling in another bullhead," he recalls, and Patrick's own line went taut. "I reeled him in and it was another one of those walking catfish," he laughs. "An even bigger one. This one was just shy of three pounds."

The Army recruiter had just beaten his own world record.

•

After twenty-four years in the military, 1st sergeant Patrick Keough gets to spend a lot of time in the outdoors. "I still love to be outside," he says. He still does a lot of hunting—ducks, turkey, deer, hogs. And he still does a lot of fishing, though he does so now from his home in Clarksville, Tennessee, a city of about 130,000 in the northwest of the Volunteer State. The headquarters of his old regiment—the Rakkasans of the 187th—is just ten miles up the road at Fort Campbell, Kentucky.

Fishing remains a passion, and aside from two world records, Keough is quite accomplished—he's got more than two certificates on his wall. He's one of fifteen anglers to be part of IGFA's Royal Bass Slam Club, which requires members to catch a largemouth, a smallmouth, a rock, a shoal, a whiterock, and a spotted bass—all to the association's standards.

And he's still working with children, this time helping to set up a duck hunt for the kids of a soldier killed in Afghanistan. Mission accomplished with his own children—and plenty of Iraqi kids, too— he thinks he might try another record.

"Once I got the first one I noticed that there are quite a lot of line-class records that can readily be broken," he says. "I'm gonna go get me a skipjack."

KING SALMON

LESTER ANDERSON, FISHERMAN

For sixteen years, Lester Anderson fished the Kenai River. The sixty-six-year-old owner of a Ford dealership, he'd make his way to the silty, glacier-blue waterway in south-central Alaska whenever he could and try his luck with the river's famous king salmon. "He worked hard all of his life, but he always made time for fun," his family would tell the *Anchorage Daily News*. "For years, summer found him up at 3 a.m. and on his beloved Kenai River by 4 a.m. so he could go to work by 8 or 9 a.m. and then go fishing again after dinner."

The mighty Kenai is perhaps the world's greatest salmon fishing arena, flowing eighty-two miles from Kenai Lake to Cook Inlet near Anderson's adopted hometown of Soldotna through the rugged and wild Kenai Peninsula. Salmon swim from one end to the other to lay their eggs in the gravel, and fishermen eagerly await them during epic migrations in June and July. The fish grow huge—bigger

Lester Anderson helped make Alaska's Kenai Peninsula one of the world's most popular salmon fishing grounds when he pulled this monster out of the Kenai River in 1985. Biologists say it would have likely weighed over one hundred pounds if he'd put it on a scale when he caught it—rather than waiting all day.
COURTESY OF THE IGFA

than anywhere else in a state famous for them—and they are close enough to the road to be accessible. The river is only one hundred miles from the state's biggest city, and Alaskans love their fishing— one in three drops a line now and again, making it the most fishing-happy state in the nation—and they line up next to the brown bears on the Kenai for a chance at the kings.

Lester Anderson landed some good size kings—or chinooks— over the years. He'd grown up in Sandy, Oregon, and moved to Alaska in 1948, a few years after he returned from World War II. He worked at Chevron until 1967 before starting a car dealership. Fishing was always on his mind. Sometimes he'd bring along his wife; sometimes he'd go with his brother-in-law, Bud. There was always a little good-natured competition. "The largest fish I caught was 63 pounds," he told the local paper. "My wife caught one 85-pounder," he said. "I could never beat her."

And then one morning in mid-May he got up early yet again to put in some time on the river before he had to hit the office and got a bite that changed his life—and the Kenai Peninsula along with it.

•

There weren't too many fishermen on the river that spring morning. Most everybody else thought it was too early in the season. The water was shallow, which made it difficult for navigation. The massive flow of meltwater from the Harding Icefield and the Kenai Mountains, which sluices down to Kenai Lake and flows on to the river itself, hadn't arrived yet. Likewise, the big runs of salmon didn't typically show up until June. Named for a northerly native tribe, the chinooks tended to swim in massive schools, appearing all at once, surging upstream in the tens of thousands. The early fish were typically smaller than the behemoths that would arrive like so many tourists in the summer. When the kings hit, the crowds did, too. But none of that mattered a whole lot to Lester Anderson. He just wanted to be out on the river.

Fishing the Kenai was popular in 1985. The banks of the river could be elbow to elbow in some well-known and easy-to-reach holes, places like the Big Eddy, Porter's Hole, Slide Hole, Poacher Cove, Sunken Island, Slikok Creek, and Centennial Park. According to the Alaska Department of Fish and Game, anglers put in more than 320,000 days on the river that year. Most of them came in June and July, though. Lester Anderson had the jump on the masses.

He and his brother-in-law, Bud Lofstedt, put their Monarch aluminum boat into the Kenai and aimed the twenty-five-horsepower motor toward Honeymoon Cove near the Kenai's Mile 13. Anderson had a variety of favorite spots on the river, as he told Louis Bignami of *Fine Fishing*. "Sometimes we'd go down to Big Eddy Hole. Other times we would fish up at Morgan's Hole. We have some spots without names, too. Big kings hang in the current around pool heads and, if you work the lure right, it'll move right along with a drifting boat to cover lots of river bottom and tempt good fish."

That day, like most days, he was working a Spin-N-Glo lure, a colorful cork body with wings that looked like a giant bumblebee. Locals called these lures "Kenai Specials," and Lester Anderson liked his particularly big. He'd add beads to them in hopes that the fish could see them through the glacial silt and aquamarine murk of the river. Anderson had his own tried-and-tested rig.

"Visitors who don't go with guides generally don't have the right gear," he explained to Bignami. "I used a big Garcia spinning reel with top-quality 25 pound test line and a special rod my buddy Clarence Wait made. Most 'Lower 48' rods don't have enough backbone for the Kenai kings."

For bait he used some salmon eggs. Then he and Lofstedt dropped their lines for the action.

They got some.

Also called chinooks, King salmon are the largest of the Pacific salmon and one of the most sought-after gamefish in the world. An anadromous species (meaning they migrate from saltwater to freshwater for breeding), they may spend as long as eight years in the ocean before returning to their spawning grounds.

A massive king took a bite—and held on. "It was about seven in the morning when I hooked the fish," Anderson told Bignami. "It immediately jumped over my brother-in-law's line. Then ran off nearly 200 yards. We had to follow it. It ran. We followed. Fortunately, we had room to work the fish. Good thing it wasn't Memorial Day. You wouldn't believe the crowds here on Memorial Day!"

The two friends spent three quarters of an hour doing battle. They finally had the fish close enough to the boat for Lofstedt to get a net on it. But the king was too big for the net and wriggled out. "I don't know how long we chased him," Anderson told the *Peninsula Clarion*. "I thought we were going to lose him. I knew it was a big one when we couldn't fit it into the net." The angler held on, though, and they were after it again, finally abandoning their boat on a sand bar. Once on land, they were able to haul the spotted beast ashore. It was so huge that the two of them had difficulty getting it back into the boat.

Then they did something most anglers couldn't even imagine after landing an epically large fish—they went back out fishing.

Anderson and Loftstedt kept at it until about eleven o'clock that morning. Once ashore, they hefted the massive fish into the back of Anderson's pickup. He had to get to work at the dealership. Anderson drove into Soldotna and went to work.

The big fish sat in the bed of the truck, one eye to the sky. That's what Anderson always did with his fish. He'd bring it home later that day and filet it up.

It sat there.

And sat there.

For seven hours.

Until someone suggested to Lester Anderson that, holy smokes, that fish was big and he ought to weigh it.

The two fishermen realized that it was big. But they assumed it was in the seventy- or eighty-pound range. A really nice catch but probably not winning enough to even challenge Anderson's wife's eighty-five-pounder. "I never really thought it was that big," Anderson told a reporter a couple years later. "I didn't even know there was a world record. I never paid attention to it."

•

There was indeed a world record. It was another Alaska king, caught by Howard Rider of Juneau eight years earlier. When Lester Anderson finally took his fish to get weighed he outweighed Rider's fish by more than four pounds. The big chinook was ninety-seven pounds four ounces, with a waist as big as a man at thirty-seven inches, and a height reaching that of a fifth grader—just shy of five feet. And it almost certainly would have topped the century mark if he'd put it on a scale immediately rather than let it dry out, evaporating, for a whole work day.

Lester Anderson was suddenly king of the king salmon.

The world certainly took notice. Since anyone could remember, the Kenai had been a favorite salmon fishery among anglers. As Lester Anderson noted, after Memorial Day it could get so cramped that it was hard to chase fish. The river grew so busy, in fact, that the Alaska state legislature created the Kenai River Special Management Area in 1984 to ensure that fishing was being done sustainably.

The landing of the world-record king—and subsequent press—made it even more crowded. "The day we caught that fish there was nobody in the hotels and restaurants," Anderson told the *Anchorage Daily News*. "The next day you couldn't get a room." That overnight timeline may have been an exaggeration, but the ultimate effect on tourism wasn't, and the president of the Kenai River Sportfishing Association, Bob Penney of Anchorage, knew it right away. On May 20, 1985, he told the *Peninsula Clarion:* "He's a lucky, lucky guy. And what a wonderful boast for the state. But that poor river will be full of people now."

He was right.

Before Lester Anderson's fateful fishing trip, there were a few dozen guide services on the Kenai Peninsula. Today, there are more than 350 guides registered with the state of Alaska, and a whole infrastructure has grown up around them. Campgrounds, lodges, and bed-and-breakfasts all cater to the tens of thousands of anglers who arrive from all over the world to try and catch a king. The restaurants and hotels did indeed fill up.

Perhaps it's all too much. Many environmentalists contend that the Kenai is overfished. Other observers say that warming temperatures are making life difficult for salmon. Everyone agrees there simply aren't as many chinooks swimming upstream, and the stats bear them out. In 2012 the run was so poor that the state's Secretary of Commerce declared a fisheries disaster in Cook Inlet, and the state turned its attention to the Kenai River.

"Kenai River Closed to All Salmon Fishing," read the headline in the July 17 *Anchorage Daily News.* "Catch and release not legal either in worst season in 30 years." The impact on the communities around the river, places like Soldotna and Cooper Landing, which depend on the arrival of wallet-toting anglers from all over the world, was simply devastating. The Alaskan government estimates that more than 730 million dollars flow into the Cook Inlet area, including the Kenai River, and that those dollars support more than eight thousand jobs. Guides everywhere were laid off. Lodges lost tens of thousands of dollars in expected income. Recreational anglers were pointing fingers at commercial fishermen who were pointing right back. "We have members calling to say they've lost 50 percent of their business in the last couple of weeks," Shanon Hamrick, executive director of the Kenai Peninsula Tourism Marketing Council, told the *Homer News.* It was bad.

Will anyone ever catch a bigger one than Lester Anderson? Hard to say. Perhaps the royal salmon of the Kenai will rebound and retake their throne.

•

Lester Anderson died in 2003 at the age of eighty-four, still the world-record holder. If he were alive today, he'd want to be able to fish, obviously, but he'd probably wish the river would quiet, becoming the sleepy wild waterway it was when he first cast into it in the late sixties, when big fish were common and you could stake out a hole and have it all to yourself. Let all the attention go somewhere else. Lester Anderson never needed all that. When he caught his massive fish he didn't bother to put it on a scale. Stuck it in the pickup and went back for more.

When he finally brought his fish to be weighed back in 1985, he had accumulated an entourage of interested people, newshounds, other anglers, photographers. At least twenty accompanied him to Echo Lake Lockers to have his catch officially recorded. He turned to a reporter and said, "All this for a fish. Can you believe it?"

7

LARGEMOUTH BASS

GEORGE PERRY, FISHERMAN
MANABU KARITA, FISHERMAN

O n a quiet stretch of US Highway 117 in Jacksonville, Georgia, is a big, black sign embossed with gold letters, standing above the tall grass. It looks like any other historic marker you might see on a roadside anywhere in America. Depending upon your interest in local history, you might or might not slow down to read it, but if you did, this is what you'd learn: "Approximately two miles from this spot, on June 2, 1932, George W. Perry, a 19-year-old farm boy, caught what was to become America's most famous fish."

Which sounds like a bit of homerism—hyperbole stoked by local pride—but in this case it's a fish tale that's not far from the truth. The twenty-two-pound largemouth bass that the boy from

The story of George Perry's 1932 world-record largemouth catch sounds like an American legend: Georgia farm boy goes fishing in his homemade boat because it's too rainy to plow, and, using his only lure, catches a twenty-two-pound large-mouth. GEORGE PERRY PHOTO, COURTESY BILL BAAB

Telfair County brought home one wet spring day at the dawn of the Depression broke the previous record by more than two pounds, and for more than seventy years it's remained king, despite the best efforts of determined fishermen across the globe.

As Monte Burke puts it in his book *Sowbelly: The Obsessive Quest for the World-Record Largemouth Bass*, the story of George Washington Perry seems like idyllic Americana. Up there with George Washington's cherry tree and Johnny Appleseed's quest, just too perfect to be true: "the circumstances—a poor farm boy, a handmade boat, a rainy washout, and the biggest bass ever recorded—make it all almost seem like a fable or a great frontier myth . . ."

It's the sort of record that you don't want to see broken.

But fishermen everywhere are gunning for it. The bigmouth bass is *the* prize catch in sportfishing—books have been written about the pursuit of this hungry member of the sunfish family, and it's estimated to be worth at least one million dollars in sponsorships. (At one point in the early part of this century a southern business consortium even offered an eight-million-dollar reward for anyone who could top Perry's catch.) But many fishing authorities said it simply couldn't be done—that they don't grow them like they used to.

That was until one summer day in July of 2009 when Manabu Karita reeled in a massive largemouth in Japan's Lake Biwa.

•

By all accounts, the largemouth is the world's most popular gamefish—and by a large margin. Southwick Associates, an outdoor market research firm, does six bimonthly surveys of recreational fishing in America each year, and every time, the bigmouth reigns. When anglers grab their fishing poles on any given day across the nation, more than half of them—55 percent—will head off in search of a largemouth bass. The next closest competitor, the poor little pan fish, sits way back at 35 percent. (Figures are from the September-October 2012 survey.) The trout, which a century ago was the piscean prince? Way down at 20 percent.

Indeed, the largemouth is responsible for some large dollars. Bass fishermen—and there are more than eleven million of them—have made their sport into a 16-billion-dollar industry, according to Southwick Associates. In Florida alone the sport is worth 1.25 billion, according to the *Miami Herald*. That's a lot of magazines, TV shows, boats, and bassmasters.

What is it that makes the largemouth king? It's got game—this black bass is a fighter. (Author of the *Book of Black Bass*, James Henshall, put it simply back in 1881: "I consider him, inch for inch, and pound for pound, the gamest fish that swims." Henshall surmised that the species would even one day overtake "the Lordly trout" in popularity.) Largemouth are both curious by nature and notoriously aggressive fish, with a predatory instinct that makes them readily take to lures and bait, which, of course, makes it fun for fishermen. Plus, they taste good. And they're prevalent, ranging all across North America.

No place, though, is the largemouth bass as revered as it is in the South, where it's the state fish in many states (Alabama, Georgia, Florida, Tennessee, and Mississippi) and the primary target of thousands of Dixie fishermen like the young George Washington Perry.

The thing is, bass seem to be getting smaller. Most state records are decades old at the least. The latest to fall was the Kansas record, when an 11.8-pounder was caught in a pond in Cherokee County in May of 2008. A few months earlier, an angler broke the Maryland record, pulling an 11.2-pounder from the Potomac River. Both of those, of course, weigh far less than Perry's. The closest comer has been a 21.2-pounder taken in California's Castaic Lake but even that was more than twenty years ago.

•

For George Perry, the day started like any other. The teenage farm boy rolled out of bed before dawn, ready to plant his fields with corn and cotton. Not yet twenty, he had lost his father about a year prior to lung cancer, and he'd shouldered more of the responsibility for keeping the family farm in operation. As Perry himself pointed out, they lived, "three creeks farther back in the woods than anyone else," and closer to the bone, too. (The banks would foreclose on their home in three years.)

But it wasn't a day for plowing or planting—rain was coming down in sheets. So George decided to see if he could put food on the family's table another way, and he went fishing with his friend Jack Page. Like just about all of his contemporaries in rural, 1930s Georgia, George Perry loved to fish for largemouth. He went over to Page's house, and they hopped into Page's 1930 Model A truck and drove down to Montgomery Lake. The small basin was simply a wide spot in the Ocmulgee River, a winding waterway that cuts 241 miles through central Georgia, draining into the coastal plain. With its lush green sides—overhung with cypress trees—it was ideal bass habitat. The fish loved to hide out among the drooping evergreen's knobby knees. Page and Perry knew just where to find them.

On this miserable morning, they weren't having much luck. Perry was at the oars of the makeshift boat they'd constructed out of barn boards. Page was plumbing the depths with their fishing rig: a pole of unknown origin and some twenty-four-pound test line, at the end of which was a Creek Chub lure (though the exact model has been a subject of much debate). Worth a princely eighty-five cents, it was the only lure they had, and, as Monte Burke points out in *Sowbelly*, they fretted every time it caught on an underwater snag. On a trip they took earlier that spring they lost the lure to a perch—it dove, snapping the line—and they turned back for shore with their heads hanging—but the fish determined the plug wasn't a snack and spat it out. Luckily, the boys heard the splash and were able to recover it.

Jack Page spent half an hour trying to turn the heads of Montgomery Lake bass to no avail on this morning, and he handed the rod off to George Perry. Perry rarely spoke about what happened next, but he's quoted as saying: "We were out to catch dinner. We only had one lure, so we shared the rod and rowing. When it was my turn, I tossed the lure back into a pocket between two fallen trees and gave the plug a couple of jerks."

In 1969, Perry gave a rare interview to *Sports Afield*, describing what happened next: "I don't remember many of the details but all at once the water splashed everywhere. I do remember striking, then raring back and trying to reel. But nothing budged. I thought for sure I had lost the fish—that he'd dived and hung me up. I had no idea how big the fish was, but that didn't matter. What had me worried was losing the lure."

It was indeed a big one, and after a "quick tussle" the two boys were able to get the bass into the boat. Both Page and Perry were truly impressed. This was not only the largest fish they'd ever caught—it was the biggest they'd ever even seen. Perry was excited to get it home and carve it up for dinner. He told *Sports Afield*: "The first thing I thought of was how nice a chunk of meat to take home."

The fish went in to a burlap bag and then into the back of the truck, and the two boys took it to the nearest scale at JJ Hall's store in the tiny hub town of Helena. The proud young anglers brought the fish into the store—bragging rights, and all—and they showed it to proprietor Jesse Hall. He was a notary public and measured and weighed the beast. It was thirty-two-and-a-half inches long, and had a twenty-eight-and-a-half-inch girth and tipped the scales at twenty-two pounds four ounces. Someone mentioned that *Field & Stream* magazine was sponsoring a big-bass competition and Perry made the quite obvious decision to enter.

Then it was off for home to filet the fish for dinner. George's mother fed the family of six that night with the first half, serving it up with onions and tomatoes and corn bread. She'd cook the other half the following evening.

George Perry would find out later that he won *Field & Stream*'s first prize: one hundred dollars worth of outdoor gear. "I remember how tickled George was when the prize package containing a new rod and reel arrived at our home," said his sister Rubye, according to author Bill Baab's authoritative chronicle of the catch, *Remembering George W. Perry*.

And more than that, he had won the world record for the largest largemouth ever landed, besting the previous record, a twenty-pound–two-ounce bass caught in Florida by Fritz Friebel in 1923. Perry enjoyed the sporting goods haul, but he was never too impressed with himself about the record. His family would later describe him as uncomfortable with all the attention.

George Perry continued fishing all of his life, but he remained unconcerned with his place in the history books. He eventually moved to Brunswick, Georgia, where he helped build Liberty Ships to fight the war. A farm boy who knew his way around tools, he proved so good at his job that the Army told him to stay home and keep at it rather than enlisting. He raised a family in Brunswick and found a new love in the coming years—aviation—and started spending a lot of time in airplane hangars, becoming a mechanic. He'd later buy his own airstrip, working as a charter pilot, and died in a plane crash in 1974.

●

For decades it looked like Perry's record was simply unbeatable. Then in the eighties, monster bass started gobbling lures in western lakes. Several Golden State basins had been stocked with a Florida strain of bass, and they seemed to be taking to their new home. One

The largemouth bass, native to North America, has an average life span of around sixteen years, though it can live longer. It's so highly prized as a gamefish that it has been introduced into other nonnative habitats, often to the detriment of the ecology.

Californian registered with IGFA two twenty-plus-pounders pulled from Lake Castaic, and the Los Angeles County reservoir became the center of the bass fishing world for a few years in the late eighties and early nineties. Lakes in Texas and Oklahoma, Alabama and Arkansas saw flurries of activity and became the next big hope among bass fishermen.

In 2003, a woman fishing from an inflatable raft in California's Spring Lake reeled in what she said was a largemouth leviathan—twenty-two pounds eight ounces. But she released it before doing any serious documentation—the kind of precise measurements, photos, and witnesses that would be required to best a seventy-year-old record. She weighed it but neglected to photograph it properly or show it to a biologist. Three years later, again in California, an angler drew what everyone thought was impossible—a twenty-five-pound largemouth—out of Dixon Lake in Escondido.

Mac Weakley of Carlsbad, California, made the *CBS News* with the catch and it quickly became something of a sensation. The fish was well documented and IGFA was prepared to consider it, when Weakley made the remarkable decision not to submit the details for world-record recognition. He was monitoring talk on the Internet about his fish and didn't like what he was reading.

Weakley gave this explanation to the *San Diego Union-Tribune*: "It seems 50 percent feel it should stand as a record and 50 percent say it shouldn't. That's why Jed (Dickerson), Mike, and I have decided not to submit it as a world record to the IGFA. We don't want to go out breaking the record with so many people doubting it. We want it to be 100 percent—or more realistically 90 percent—being behind it with no controversy."

And there was controversy. Weakley foul-hooked the fish—he caught it below its dorsal fin rather than in its mouth—which is considered illegal in California. He also let her go. This particular bass was a known commodity—Weakley and his buddies had even hooked the distinctive fish before—and anglers all over descended on the lake to try their hand at nabbing "Dottie" when they heard Weakley's story. (Known by a black stripe beneath her right gill plate, she's since been found floating on the surface, apparently dead of natural causes.)

Bass fever spread across the globe.

Manabu Karita most certainly was aware of Dottie. A native of Japan, he was keen on finding world-record largemouth. But the species was relatively rare in his home country, existing in only a few locations. So he did what he had to do to find the fish, as he told the website TackleTour in February 2010: "When I was 3 or 4 years old, my grandfather used to take me skink and carp fishing, but I began bass fishing maybe 19 years ago. At that time, there were hardly any bass to be found in Japan, so my friend and I had to ride a bicycle 100 km [62 miles] one way to fish for them."

He found them in Lake Biwa, Japan's largest freshwater lake, a 258-square-mile basin near the city of Kyoto. Surrounded by mountains and famous for its clarity, the lake supplies drinking water to more than fifteen million people in south central Japan. Biwa is beloved by beachgoers, tourists, pleasure boaters and—thanks to fifty-eight species of fish—fishermen. Any given weekend, Karita told TackleTour, might see him competing with three to five hundred other boats for their attention. The largemouth is considered a *gaijin*—an invasive foreigner—and they aren't allowed to be dropped back overboard live. No catch and release here. It's capture and kill.

In 2002, Manabu Karita started to get very serious about this delicious outsider. Like so many other fishermen, he had a zeal that was almost obsessive. "Three hundred sixty five days a year, when I'm fishing, when I'm driving, when I'm with friends, I always think about world-record bass," he told TackleTour.

Karita fished at every opportunity and experimented with gear. "Part of my preparation is making sure to always use new hooks and line." He tried fishing both fast and slow, looked for both seasonal and native bass, and used different types of bait, like gill and sweetfish, strategies based on his keen observation of fish behavior and the "intuition" that he developed.

In July 2009, he was back at Lake Biwa, fishing with hundreds of others. This summer day, he was encouraged by the sight of a school of twenty-pound bass. "I see schools like this 2 or 3 times a year," he told TackleTour, "with each school having around seven fish."

He had twenty-five-pound Toray Super Hard line on his Shimano Antares reel, on a Dops Side winder rod, and he was fishing in about fifteen feet of water. The angler put a bit of bluegill bait on his rod and dropped it over the side. He felt a hit and fought the "high-spirited fish" for about three minutes before he was able to pull it into the boat. Karita was immediately impressed by its size, but he kept fishing anyway. When he finally put it on a scale, Karita discovered that his bigmouth weighed twenty-two pounds four ounces—heftier than George Perry's untouchable world-record bass by a whopping .03 kilograms.

•

Manabu Karita's dedication paid off. It took some time, but the Japanese angler's catch was certified by IGFA—He has officially tied George Perry's elusive record. Technically his catch weighed more, but IGFA's rules state that it has to surpass the current record by 0.5 percent, and so he gets a share of the spoils.

Kurita was invited to visit Montgomery Lake when he made a tour of the United States in 2011, and he met George's son. According to author Bill Baab, the world's foremost authority on Perry's catch, Kurita was struck by the spot where the young Georgian made history. "It was a revelation," says Baab. "He caught his fish in a lake that's probably two hundred feet deep. George caught his in a mudhole."

Baab says Perry wouldn't be disappointed at all in having his record matched. "Records are made to be broken. George would have been the first to congratulate the Japanese kid. He was a really nice boy." When the record finally does fall, Baab says, he wants it to go to a kid like Kurita or a young man from Georgia out fishing for the day. "I want it to be caught by someone like George rather than one of these elite bass fishermen."

But for now the world record of a Georgia farm boy—who caught a massive fish, casting from a handmade boat with his only lure because it was too rainy to plow—endures.

8

RAINBOW TROUT
ADAM AND SEAN KONRAD, FISHERMEN

They broke out more than a decade ago, escaping through a neat little hole. It was a mass exodus, more than half a million prisoners shoving and bumping each other in a rush to get out. Merging with the native population in seconds, the "ex-cons" made recapture all but impossible. And then they simply dispersed in the dark, assimilating, trying to live a normal life on the outside.

Until the day Adam Konrad caught one.

A twenty-six-year-old auto mechanic from Saskatoon, Saskatchewan, Konrad was fishing the province's famous man-made Lake Diefenbaker one June day when he reeled in an astonishingly large rainbow trout—a 28.3-pound beauty. It was a new provincial record—but not quite as big as the ten-pound-line-class world-record rainbow caught on the same lake two years prior by Duane

Adam Konrad had the world record for rainbow trout (43.6 pounds) for only two years before it was beaten—by his own twin brother, Sean, who caught a 48-pounder. The pair fish together in Saskatchewan's Lake Diefenbaker, where more than half a million triploid trout—farm-grown fish with a third chromosome that makes them grow big—escaped into the wild in 2000. Many fisherman say that the third chromosome makes the Konrads' records illegitimate. COURTESY OF THE IGFA

Farden. That one weighed 30.6 pounds. Not long after, Adam's identical twin, Sean, landed a big one too. Between the two of them, the Konrad brothers hauled in a stream of giants during the span of three weeks. After the 28-pound fish came a 30-pounder and then the grande dame—these were all female fish—a 33.3-pounder.

The Konrads kept coming back, driving the eighty-five miles from their homes in Saskatoon to fish "Lake Dif." And they kept pulling in massive fish, until Adam hooked a 43.6-pound rainbow and beat the world record.

•

Turns out there was a reason all these fish were so huge. They were escapees from CanGro Fish Farm, an aquaculture operation that raised genetically engineered rainbows in pens at the head of Diefenbaker. CanGro raises more than two million pounds of rainbow meat each year. These are special fish bred for the restaurant market, and they are not like their common cousins. Known as triploids, they have three chromosomes rather than the usual two, which renders them sterile. "They don't reproduce, therefore they can put more energy into their growth," says Norm Dyck, a fisheries biologist for the Province of Saskatchewan. "That's basically why they can get so big." Indeed, the fish are famous for eating and eating and eating and growing and growing and growing.

The triploids escaped that fateful night in 2000 when a big piece of ice tore a hole in their containment pen. More than five hundred thousand "wildwest steelhead," as the company called them, swam off that evening and began new lives as Diefenbaker gamefish.

Gamefish on steroids, as some complained. When Adam Konrad was recognized as a world-beater by the International Game Fish Association, a firestorm of protest followed. Many anglers thought that Konrad's fish should have been disqualified because it was commercially grown, just as the governing bodies of other sports reject athletes who use steroids. "IGFA seems ready to hand over world records to anyone who can produce a Frankenfish," wrote one. "That fish is an artificially created monster. I hope they don't recognize genetically engineered fish to be legitimate world records . . ." wrote another.

Just like its population of controversial rainbows, Lake Diefenbaker is a creation of man, coming into existence in 1967 when the South Saskatchewan and the Qu'Appelle Rivers were dammed. And just like its rainbows, the lake is massive, a long slender finger that stretches for more than 140 miles. Fishermen flock to its 500 miles of shoreline, sinking lines into the depths—some 217 feet of them—in search of everything from trout to walleye. "If Lake Diefenbaker is famous for one thing," say the tourism brochures, "that would be its first-class fishing." Everyone, it seems, loves "the Jewel of the Prairies."

Biologist Norm Dyck, who occasionally introduces walleye fish fry into Diefenbaker, doesn't remember the lake being a particularly good rainbow fishery before the CanGro accident. "There always are some rainbow trout that come down from the Bow River area in Alberta. They're stocked higher up the river. And you'd hear of the odd big rainbow before, but it wasn't a great fishery for rainbow trout." Since word hit the Internet that there were unnaturally large rainbows in "Lake Dif," however, the place has been boiling with fishermen.

●

"We've been fishing Diefenbaker since we were six years old," says Adam Konrad. "Like any other kids, our dad always took us fishing." Their father, Otto, was a real estate agent, and they'd pack off for a day—or a weekend—at the lake, rods in hand. The twins enjoyed these father-son camping trips, but they didn't become passionate about fishing until adolescence hit.

"My father had taken us fishing one time," recalls Adam, "and we'd seen this big pike under the boat. It was thirty pounds or so, and we wondered why we couldn't catch fish like that. We were twelve or thirteen." Like a pair of Ahabs, they decided that pike would be theirs. "We figured out where he'd be—and we hooked him."

All it took was one big fish—the boys were hooked as well. "After that we'd pick a bay, and we'd catch one big pike after another." Throughout their high school years, they'd fish whenever they could, and they got even more serious after they got their driver's licenses. College came—Adam went off to three years of engineering school—and the pair took jobs as service technicians for Hyundai in Saskatoon.

Fishing remained a favorite pastime and the brothers would make the pilgrimage from Saskatoon to Diefenbaker often in search of ever bigger fish. They'd tried different spots on the lake, and had a fair amount of success, hooking ten- to twelve-pound rainbows, but they never reeled in anything more impressive. They'd talk to the other fishermen they'd see, and they heard that these small trout were nothing like some of the others being landed. "We started hearing that a thirty-pounder was caught and we wondered how. We started talking to more people and doing research," Adam recalls.

Like fishermen anywhere, many of the anglers they spoke to were loath to divulge their secrets. But one gregarious fellow told them they should head over to the tail race—the area at the head of the massive reservoir where the big turbines of Gardiner dam churned—and try fishing there. The Konrads were dubious. "We didn't believe there could be big rainbows there," Adam says. They gave it a go anyway, making a dozen trips to the big dam. "My brother hooked one, probably fifteen pounds, and it was the biggest one we'd gotten."

That fish proved to them that big rainbows were beneath the depths, and they kept after them. The fish they pulled out of the tail race got bigger and bigger and as they grew, so did the Konrads' desire to catch an even larger one. The twins set a goal of breaking the Provincial record—27.5 pounds—and it became almost obsessive. "We'd go at least four times a week," says Adam. Weekends for the two mechanics would be marathon sessions. The pair would fish all of Saturday and all through Saturday night and then all day Sunday—sleep be damned.

The bigger the trout, the bigger their need to cast again. They set their sights higher. "Our goal was to break every line-class rainbow-trout record," says Adam. "We kind of dedicated everything to it. I had two or three credit cards maxed out for gas money and tackle. I didn't have a girlfriend—I couldn't have a girlfriend, I was fishing all the time."

Work at anything long enough and you get good at it. "You gotta know what you're doing," says fisheries biologist Norm Dyck of Lake Diefenbaker. "And these two—the Konrad brothers—have it figured out. For almost anything that swims, they know how to catch it."

Indeed, the twins soon learned the secrets of the tail race. It was elementary biology—and the trick known by all good fishermen. "You gotta learn how big, fat fish are going to eat," says Adam. "And you gotta learn where they're going to swim."

The Konrads caught ever-larger fish—"we were catching five or ten twenty-pound rainbows per day. I can't even count how many rainbows over twenty pounds I've caught —[probably] five hundred to a thousand," says Adam. Not only rainbows but other giants as well: lake trout weighing thirty-plus pounds, pikes north of twenty pounds, walleye over ten. But they could only see rainbows—the colorful fish were their passion—And the records began to fall.

There was that dramatic day in June 2006 when the Konrads were fishing from either side of their boat, and each felt a heavy bite. Sean reeled his in, and Adam jokingly told him to let it go because he had a bigger one. ("We always compete with each other," says Adam, "but we always work as a team. That's how we outfish all those other people.") Bigger indeed. When he finally pulled it into the boat he found he had a beast—thirty-four inches long and 28.45 pounds, breaking the Provincial record by about a pound. Soon fish like this—and broken records—became old hat. "We broke the line-class record three times in three weeks," says Adam. The following weekend Sean hauled up a thirty-pounder.

Now, they were looking to beat the world. They would need a rainbow weighing more than 42.2 pounds to best a fish caught off Alaska's Bell Island in 1970 by David White. But they were convinced they could do it. The following weekend they took a step closer.

Adam reeled in their first world-record fish. He and Sean were back at their preferred spot, and they'd brought along their best friends, Shane and Ben. After about three hours, Adam cast for the umpteenth time, waited, and then came a hit that would change his life. It felt big. "As it came out of the water on its first jump, all our mouths dropped at its size," Adam described on his website. The fish took about fifty yards of line in ten seconds. "It eventually started to tire, and we realized that our net was not nearly big enough to fit the head of the rainbow." The pair were glad they brought along their buddies because they needed the muscle. "It was a good thing we had extra bodies there because Ben had to hold Sean's legs down in the boat while he reached in and hoisted the beast into our boat." The fish was indeed a biggie—33.3 pounds, thirty-eight inches—good enough for a world record for the twelve-pound-line class.

A year later, in June 2007, the twins were back again in their favorite place, having left work after a long day. They'd brought along their friend, Tyler. Adam and Tyler were working a walleye hole. Sean was casting for rainbows. He hooked one eighteen-pounder. "After releasing the fish, I was about to check on my brother to see how they were making out with the walleye. I decided to cast out a few more times before taking a break."

It was a good decision.

Adam described the catch on his site: "I launched my Mepps Syclops into the air and slowed down my lure presentation in order to focus on the lure movement. Just as it started working properly, I felt the thump on the line. I set the hook quickly, but the fish wouldn't move. Knowing I had put the maximum tension on my 6 pound test line, I loosened my drag and waited. I felt one tail wag, then another, and over the next minute the fish refused to move. I called to Sean in anticipation that another thirty-plus pounder might be on my line. Something felt different about this fish: the brute force of it was amazing.

"As I finally pulled the monster from his feeding lie, I could feel him rolling," Adam continues. "Keeping pressure on the fish, I began to tire. My arms were burning and were still tired from the lengthy fight with the 18-pounder. Keeping my line in the air as high as possible, I yelled out to Sean again, '30 pounder!' Something did not feel right about this fish. The way it fought was different, much different, than our previous 30 pounders."

Finally, Sean came to his brothers' aid, bringing with him a scale, a tape, and a video camera. Adam dueled with the fish for another twelve minutes before catching sight of its belly. "The fish came about forty feet in front of me when I saw its size. It was unbelievable, and I instantly knew it was the largest rainbow I'd ever seen. Realizing that my dream fish might be on the other end of the line, I quickly loosened my drag—there was no way I was letting one strong tail wag snap my line like so many times in the past."

After fighting for ten more minutes the fish finally gave up and Adam sprinted into the water and grabbed him. "As I lifted him out of the water and felt the dead weight of the fish, my arms went numb and my mind went blank. I had no words to say, but I knew my goal had been reached."

Adam Konrad had a new world record: 43.6 pounds.

Aggressive feeders and balletic performers once they're on your line, rainbow
trout are prized by fishermen wherever they make an appearance.

•

With the record, their reputation spread even farther. So many people began approaching them that it eventually dawned on the Konrads that they could potentially make some money guiding. They set up their own guide service, Fishing Geeks, and began taking clients to their secret fishing hole.

"We guided for three years, and then Sean caught that fish," says Adam, referring to his brother's 2009 forty-eight-pounder, which topped Adam's 2007 fish, becoming the new world record.

"How was that possible? Any of our clients could have caught that fish. The odds of that happening . . ." he trails off.

•

Triploids. Triploids. Triploids. After setting their world records, that's all the Konrads heard about. How their fish were about as legitimate as Barry Bonds's home-run record or Marion Jones's gold medals. "That ain't no real rainbow, it's a genetically altered freak . . . that said, I'd love to reel that SOB in," said one online pundit. Tom Cushman of *Trout Underground* agreed: "New genetically engineered rainbow trout smashes record of old genetically engineered rainbow trout (yawn)," he wrote. Amazon's "Askville" made the question: "Is the 48 Pound Trout Pulled from Lake Diefenbaker Legitimate or a Hoax?" one of their daily debates, and it spurred much commentary both pro and con. Even *Wired* magazine weighed in with the headline, "48-Pound Trout: World Record or Genetic Cheat?"

Message boards scrolled on and on ad infinitum: These are not real fish. These are real fish. "Bravo. Good catch. Genetic? Please," says one. "No one will stand a chance to break the record if genetically altered fish are permitted," says another. The arguments were long and persuasive on both sides and grew in sophistication. Many felt that what they were doing was a) legal under the rules and b) open to anyone who could catch one that large. Others felt that this was simply not natural and that genetically modified fish had no place in such a traditional sport.

Fisheries biologist Norm Dyck heard fishermen grumbling around Saskatchewan too. "There was a fair bit of talk up here about it being a triploid and therefore it shouldn't count," he says. But as an outdoorsman himself, he's torn. "They have worked at it. They are avid fishermen, and they know what they're doing. They've spent hours and hours and days and days out there." So, in a way, they've earned it. The fish have also been certified by IGFA, "and that's good enough for me," says Dyck. "I've never caught anything remotely that big."

On the other hand, Dyck sees certain similarities to his preferred sport. "I'm a deer hunter, and I look at the Internet and see the YouTube videos with deer hunters and their kills. Some of these deer are raised on game farms, and they want to call them world records. I'm sure they're fed with steroids, and that doesn't seem legitimate to me at all. But triploid fish. I don't know . . ."

Adam Konrad found all the talk and his rising celebrity fascinating. He would regularly stay up late reading about himself online. "The emails and stuff were almost addicting," he says.

After the catch, ESPN asked him to do a live chat online, and he knew the question was coming. "My Dad said, 'they're going to ask you about triploids.' And they did. And he didn't have much to say at the time. His comeback for a time was, "go catch a world record then."

But Adam Konrad thinks there's more to Lake Diefenbaker's rainbows than a third chromosome. He's been reluctant to share what he believes is the truth, not wanting to pull back the curtain, not wanting to divulge the phenomenon creating monster rainbows, not wanting to spoil the fishery. But he feels the spot is being overrun already. *Outdoor Canada* already published the exact location in 2012, and fishermen have been flocking to it like seagulls to a lobster boat.

"Sean and I fished two or three years to find that spot," Adams says. "We ended up figuring it out." Now everyone knows. "To be honest, the fishing pressure that spot gets is retarded," says Adam.

The brothers themselves have felt pressure as well. They've been taken advantage of by lawyers, and they have their own stalkers. "People will try to follow us around," says Adam. It grew so bad they had to change their habits. "We switched to night-time so they couldn't see where we're fishing, what we're using."

One of these secretive angling expeditions to Lake Dif yielded Sean another world record—a twenty-five-pound–two-ounce burbot (otherwise known as a cusk) in March of 2010. This fish was probably not genetically altered.

Since then, the Konrads have seen their enthusiasm for chasing giganta-fish wane somewhat. Sean Konrad has moved hours away to Alberta. Both of the twins have married and have small girls. Gone are the days when they can go to Diefenbaker four times a week. These days, it's an occasional thing. "We'll get together and fish every couple of weeks now," says Adam. "After having a kid, your priorities change." Still, angling is always on their minds. "The wives hate it when we get together. All we talk about is fishing."

So, Adam Konrad thinks the world might be ready to know the truth behind Lake Diefenbaker's legendary rainbows. The CanGro triploids had something to do with it, sure. "But 90 percent of the fish from the pens are dead," he says. The real reason is not genetically engineered fish, though, according to Konrad, but the turbines of Gardiner Dam. It's simple, really. "When water comes out it's all churned and aerated," he says. And the water is cold, coming up from one hunded feet below, where the warming rays of the sun don't hit. Rainbow trout love cool water with a high oxygen content. "It's kind of ideal conditions," says Konrad.

There's more, though. Water isn't the only thing getting churned. "The fish come through turbines and get all chopped up," Adam explains. "The rainbows will sit and eat chum, and they can pretty much eat all day, unlimited. People think it's the triploids—but it's the food source. They're really smart fish."

9

LONGNOSE GAR

TOWNSEND MILLER, FISHERMAN

ownsend Miller was a man with a double life. That was the gist of a feature that the *Chicago Tribune* ran in 1976, comparing the Austin, Texas, legend with Clark Kent and Walter Mitty. When the sun was high, Townsend Miller went to work like everybody else, taking to his desk and telephone at Merrill, Lynch, Pierce, Fenner, and Smith in Texas's capital, watching what was happening on Wall Street and buying and selling stocks accordingly. He dressed the part, acted the part, and was by most accounts good at his job.

When darkness overtook Austin, however, an entirely different Townsend Miller could be found haunting the city's legendary nightclubs. In the late seventies Austin, Texas, was rightly famous as home to one of the nation's hippest music scenes, where, as Townsend put it, "rednecks and longhairs," could be found "side by side, drinkin' and dancin'" to a variety of country known as "cosmic

With its scaly sides, long body, and toothy snout, the longnose gar seems like a prehistoric cousin of the alligator, and it fights like one too. Famous Austin music writer Townsend Miller became fascinated by the fish when one launched itself at his chest when he was a boy, and he caught this six-foot, 50.3-pound beast in Texas's Trinity River in 1954. COURTESY OF THE IGFA

strum and twang." This was the time when "outlaw" country artists like Waylon Jennings and Willie Nelson were rocking clubs and incubating a whole scene outside the suffocating influence of Nashville.

And Townsend Miller was the king of the night, flitting from club to club, covering all the action for the *Austin American-Statesman*, hobnobbing with the stars. His daily column became the who's who and what's what of the city, a must read even for people who didn't care so much for picking and partying. Nelson called him "one of the giants of country music."

The *Chicago Tribune* was indeed correct that Townsend Miller was a Renaissance man—Miller himself once said that he "packed two days and two nights into every twenty-four hours." And he certainly led multiple lives. But the venerable newspaper missed a few. The Austin scenester didn't just lead a double life. He led a half dozen lives. The paper didn't mention his harmonica playing. Or his obsession with baseball.

Or the fact that he was a national authority on fishing for the prehistoric-looking cousin to the dinosaurs known as gar. His knowledge of gar fishing led zoos to ask for his help capturing fish and *Sports Illustrated* to ask him out for a day on the water.

At the time of the *Tribune* piece Townsend Miller held the world record for longnose gar.

He still does.

•

The fish in question was massive—six feet one-half inch and 50.31 pounds looks unusual with the toothy smile of a crocodile—the kind of river monster that you wouldn't want to meet when you're taking a relaxing dip. Long and skinny, and with a protruding needle nose, gar are considered trash fish by many fishermen, repulsive to look at and unappetizing—not to mention the fact that their eggs are poisonous and their skin is hard and armored. Native tribes used their scales to make breastplates and arrowheads; early farmers used them to make plows. The homely critters bask in rivers and lakes all across North America, but find the warm, shallow, vegetated waters of the American South ideal habitat. Alabama, North Carolina, and the Mississippi watershed are particular favorites. And they just love Miller's home state of Texas.

The gar is an unusual creature for a variety of reasons, not the least of which is that it's a fish with an extra lung that allows it to breathe like a gator—it can often be seen lifting its snout to take a sniff of air. (This is a luxury, however, because it has gills that process oxygen for it just as any other species of fish.) Needlenose gar are so reminiscent of alligators that one of the more popular species of gar is named after the fearsome reptiles.

Many of the anglers who fish for gar—especially alligator gar—do so in the shallows with spear and bow, and some genuine beasts have been taken this way. Bow hunters have shot alligator gar as big as actual alligators—365 pounds in one case. In Texas, longnose as big as 80 pounds have been harvested with an arrow. Bowhunting alligator gar is a tradition in Louisiana, where the meat is considered a delicacy. Other gar hunters snare them in nets.

The longnose—aka the Billfish, Billy Gar, or needle-nose—will also rise to live bait, and despite their reputation as undesirables, they've been preyed upon enough by humans to endanger their populations in many places. They've survived nearly one hundred million years only to be nearly extirpated in many places—they're considered threatened in South Dakota, Pennsylvania, and Delaware, for example.

Townsend Miller both contributed to the problem—he landed hundreds of gar in a lifetime of fishing—and was a part of the solution, thanks to his wealth of knowledge of the animals. A native of Gainesville, a small city near the Oklahoma border, Miller was fascinated by gar ever since one slammed into his midriff when he was a boy. He'd been wading in waist-deep water, fishing contentedly, when a gar took his bait. He instinctively yanked back on his line and the fish launched through the air onto his stomach, making his acquaintance. And that was it. He might have hooked it, but it captured him.

Born in 1919, the young Miller took to hunting and fishing early and with the same sort of zeal he had for baseball and country music. When he wasn't sitting at home listening to the Light Crust Doughboys on local radio, he was probably at one of his favorite holes along the Trinity River, a 710-mile waterway that carves its way through East Texas, flowing from the border with Oklahoma all the way to the sea at Trinity Bay. The river starts to pick up steam right near Miller's hometown, and he always loved to fish the Elm Fork between his home in Gainesville and Grapeland and Crockett, down near Dallas. Along this eighty-five-mile stretch, the Trinity is shallow and slow, flowing through wooded bottomlands that offer an ideal environment for a variety of birds and beavers, musk turtles and diamondback water snakes. And, of course, gar.

After a boyhood of hunting and fishing, watching baseball and studying the traditional sounds emanating from radios across Texas, he went off to prestigious Rice University in 1937, putting in four interrupted years. He joined the Army Air Corps when war broke out and left for western Europe, where he served as a navigator on a B17 with the 487th Bomb Group of the 8th Army Air Force Division. Upon returning home in 1944, he enrolled in North Texas State University's journalism program.

After graduation, Miller found a job that seemed perfect for him—editor at *Texas Game and Fish* magazine (which would eventually morph into *Texas Parks and Wildlife*), a state-run publication. He spent years at his desk there, reporting on all that was going on in the world of hunting and fishing—and he relished every opportunity to get out into the field. He'd get to his favorite spots along the Elm Fork as often as he could and wouldn't hesitate to travel either, checking out the gar fishery in places like the White River in Arkansas. He once hauled in a seven-foot–six-inch alligator gar that weighed in at 165 pounds. Miller explained in a *Texas Parks and Wildlife* profile that fishing for gar was a numbers game for him—he expected to be able to hook about half that took his bait and to land a third of those.

The big one came in the summer of 1954, when he was thirty-five years old. Of course, he was fishing the Trinity, working a hole in the small community of Granbury. Miller was still casting on a July day, sending his line into about twenty feet of water. According to *Texas Parks and Wildlife*, the angler usually liked to use a saltwater rig, with a #6/0 treble hook, a six-foot steel leader, a seventy-pound test line, and a heavy swivel. In this case he was using an Actionrod, with a Penn reel, and Ashaway line. His working method was to scan the river searching for surfacing gar, and when he saw activity, anchor and drop his line to the bottom. On one of the hooks of his treble he'd attach a piece of bait—the record was caught on gaspergou. On the others he would crimp the barbs to prevent the gar from biting the line and spitting out the hook. The bent barbs would better catch in the hard bony snout. (Catch-and-release advocates suggest a circular hook, which only sticks the corner of their beak and does less damage to the fish.)

On this particular July day, he felt a heavy hit and let the fish swim away to swallow the bait and set the hook. He then proceeded to fight the gar for more than fifteen minutes. Longnose gar are among the more combative freshwater species—they'll fight and launch themselves like missiles—and that combined with their size leads to some epic battles. When Townsend Miller finally landed his fish he must have known instantly that it was something special—it was the longest longnose he'd ever seen, more than six feet long, with a waistline like a first-grader and fifty pounds of heft.

(This wasn't Miller's first record-breaking fish. In 1951, he'd landed a spotted bass while fishing in Lake Texoma. Weighing in at four pounds four ounces, it was a Texas state record that would hold for almost two decades before falling in 1970.)

Also known as the needlenose gar, longnose gar are a kind of living fossil. Based on the evidence, gar have been present in certain habitats for at least one hundred million years.

Miller's reputation as a gar fisherman spread far and wide. *Sports Illustrated* came calling a month after his catch to do a feature for its second ever issue, calling him a man who has "dedicated his life to gar fishing and gar study." Miller went tarpon fishing in the Gulf of Mexico with writer Hart Stilwell, and the Gainesville native told the *SI* writer that he'd always called the gar "inland tarpon," because both had armor, bony snouts, and would fly when hooked.

Though they started off looking for tarpon, Miller and Stilwell ended up landing alligator gar. The pair entered a friendly competition with some Gulf fishermen who used small sailing rafts to chase gar, using tarpon as bait. When they scored a fish, they'd cut it open with an ax and fry the meat. Stillwell called it a cross between a french fry and a chitlin—"smells awful," he wrote, "but tastes all right."

These locals told Miller and Stilwell they couldn't possibly catch alligator gar on the plugs they were using. The pair took the bait, finding a murky sandbar where they could see gar in the shallows. "Within two minutes Miller had a big one." The writer offered it up to the astonished locals. He caught several more "not a one under five feet." The next day the Gulf fishermen were lined up on the bank hoping that Miller would catch more gar for them.

Other adventures awaited. Because of his deep understanding of the fish, he was asked by the Fort Worth Zoo to help land a live alligator gar for the zoo's menagerie. He assembled a crack team that included zoo curator Lawrence Curtis, Miller's longtime fishing buddy Jeff Krenek, and Miller's six-year-old son, Kent. Off they went to his beloved Trinity, nabbing the zoo a "small" specimen, 148 pounds and just shy of seven feet long.

•

In April of 1983, Townsend Miller wrote his last column for the *Statesman*. He could still be seen around town at big country shows, nipping into a flask full of "Townsend's Treacherous Treat" a concoction made of vodka and crème de menthe, and he was famous enough that the cameras would follow him whenever he visited the set of PBS's *Austin City Limits*.

Six years later he'd be found dead in a burned car near a local lake. Authorities ruled his death an accident, guessing that the long grass under the vehicle caught fire—cigarette or engine malfunction—and consumed him before he could escape. He was sixty-nine.

Upon his tragic passing in 1989, Townsend Miller was inducted into the Western Swing Hall of Fame, and more than eight thousand clippings, photographs, and recordings of country stars were donated to the University of Texas for the Townsend Miller Collection. The Kerville Music Foundation and the Austin Community College's Commercial Music Management Program also set up scholarships in his name to support worthy up-and-comers. As someone once quipped, if there were a Gar Fishing Hall of Fame, he'd be the first inductee.

Tributes poured out when Miller died. Monte Warden of the Wagoneers said, "he was and still will be Austin country music, the heart and soul of it . . ." Country legend Doug Sahm said simply: "An era of Austin has left with him."

And one reporter wrote in the *Statesman*: "Remember the enthusiasm you had as a kid? When you never ran out of energy for fear you might miss something? Townsend Miller, who died last Saturday morning at age sixty-nine, seemed to always have that level of energy."

10

BROWN TROUT

TOM HEALY, FISHERMAN
ROGER HELLEN, FISHERMAN

"When I arrived, I thought they were going to crown me mayor of Manistee." The day was a momentous one for Tom Healy. The retired contractor had just landed a forty-one-pound-seven-ounce brown trout in the Manistee River and had pulled in to the small Michigan town of the same name. The fish was a special one. It had undoubtedly beaten the state record and may well have been a world beater, too, and whether or not that was the case, a crowd had gathered to see it. "There were probably two dozen people waiting for us," Healy says. "That was about ten o' clock in the morning. I was there until four in the afternoon."

Tom Healy, his guide, and his friend Bob Woodhouse, set up in front of Pier Pressure Charters downtown and showed the fish to

Michigan angler Tom Healy (top) caught a forty-one-pound–seven-ounce brown trout in the Manistee River near the Michigan town of the same name in 2009, only to have it challenged ten months later by a forty-one-pound–eight-ounce brownie reeled in by Wisconsinite Roger Hellen (bottom) in Lake Michigan.
COURTESY OF THE IGFA

all comers, shaking hands and hefting the massive salmonid for pictures. Everyone wanted to see this giant trout, get a snapshot taken with it, hear the fisherman tell the tale of the fight. Pictures show the sixty-seven-year-old Healy with his elbows braced against his side, his face red, like a weight lifter doing curls, straining to hold the fish up for yet another photo. He barely had time to call his wife, Cathy, and tell her the good news.

"My guide Tim Roller said to me, 'Shouldn't you call your wife?'" Healy recalls with a laugh. That was about noon. Healy left her a message: "This isn't a joke. I'm standing here in downtown Manistee and I've caught a record-breaking fish." They finally connected a couple of hours later. By then his astonishing catch was already old news. "I know," his wife Cathy told him. "It's all over the place."

The story was much the same with his son, Sean. He'd been out golfing when one of his buddies said to him, "Is your dad Tom Healy? Was he fishing today?" The news lit up with broadcasts about Healy and his brown trout.

"By the time I got home the phone was ringing off the hook."

Small towns, big fish.

Tom Healy was stunned by it all. A self-effacing retiree, he simply wanted a quiet day of fishing. "What really touched me, though, was how much respect the people of Manistee gave that fish," he says. "That community, their whole livelihood has to do with fishing and the outdoors."

And, indeed, the town of six thousand bills itself as the "fishing capital of the Midwest"—perhaps a bit of hyperbole, but one based on facts. With easy access to Lake Michigan and Manistee Lake, there is world-class fishing right off its docks. According to a 2009 *Field & Stream* article, more state-record fish have been caught near the convergence of the two than anywhere else in Michigan. Several brown trout larger than thirty pounds have been caught off the pier in town. The larger Manistee County is home to three of the five nationally designated wild and scenic rivers in the state's Lower

Peninsula—the Big Manistee among them—and boasts almost three hundred miles of waterway.

So Manistee has some bragging rights, and Tom Healy has been a regular visitor. The town is about an hour and a half from his home in Rockford, Michigan, and he has spent hours and hours and days and days fishing nearby with guide Tim Roller.

Healy was overwhelmed by the response of the community to his big brown. When it was a confirmed world record, besting the forty-pound–four-ounce brownie caught by Howard Collins in Arkansas's Little Red River in 1992, big-box outfitter Cabelas made him six models in exchange for others to display in their stores. Grafeful, Healy promptly gave one to the people of Manistee.

All the attention was a bit much for the family man from the small town of Rockford. For Tom Healy it's always been about the trout. He doesn't think having pulled a fish from a river makes him any sort of superhero. "I love to talk about the fish," he says, "but I don't want to come across as bragging. It's not about me, it's about the fish. I've been a very lucky fisherman."

Lucky perhaps, but, as the saying goes, luck will only take you so far. Healy's been doing it so long he's learned many tricks and techniques, and this has resulted in some fine catches. He has a room full in his home that he calls his "dry aquarium." In 1963 when he was in college at Michigan Tech, he pulled up a forty-six-inch pike. Four years later, he snagged a nineteen-pound–four-ounce steelhead. In 2000 he went brook trout fishing in Labrador and caught several big brookies weighing six and a half pounds or more. The ever-cooperative Manistee yielded up a thirteen-pound–six-ounce walleye in 2004. On his annual bone fishing trip to the Bahamas he reeled in a twelve-pound-five-ounce bone.

"All of that is lucky," he says. His friend Bob Woodhouse, who was fishing with him on that day in September, told CNN there definitely was a lot more to it than luck. Perseverance. Determination. "Tom's worked, he's fished on this river for forty years or more and he deserves it. He's put in a million casts to earn this fish."

Healy: "Of course, there's *some* skill involved."

For Tom Healy, it's a skill that dates back to the fifties when he was a boy in Grand Rapids. "I got involved with fly-tying in the Boy Scouts," he recalls. "I was twelve or thirteen and got a book and practiced tying flies." He earned his merit badge, and he figured the next logical step was to get a fly rod and try out the flies he made. Could he actually land a trout on one of his homemade ties? The eager angler had an uncle who was happy to take him.

"My dad was not a big fisherman, but my uncle lived on a lake, and we'd go up and fish from his boat. My other uncle loved to go ice fishing." Whether from the rail of a boat or through a hole in the lake, it didn't matter to the young Tom—he just wanted to go fishing.

Healy kept at it until he went to high school, where he found some buddies who also liked to wet a line. One of them had a car, and they'd all go off on angling adventures. "That's probably where the seeds of this passion came from," he says. College took him north to the Upper Peninsula, where he learned how to fish for steelheads. Salmon are his favorite species of all.

For decades Healy fished whenever he could, but there was competition from a wife, four kids, and a career managing a construction company. Now retired, Healy has all the time in the world to fish, and he takes full advantage. The Michigan angler spends at least a couple of months a year fishing somewhere for something, and there's a certain rhythm to his year.

"Serious fishing begins in late August and runs through the beginning of December," he says. "Spring fishing in March and April. And then bone fishing in the Bahamas in May." He doesn't really care too much for fishing in the heat of summer—and the fishing isn't particularly good then, anyway. "But I might take the grandkids—five girls, two boys—fishing for bluegills and perch from the dock at the lake in the summer."

All this time spent angling has given Healy a depth of experi-ence that few fishermen can equal. Friendly and knowledgeable, he'd make a great guide, but usually still hires someone to take him out. "Things can change in a day," he says. "Since the guides are there every day they know exactly what's happening and where to go. To own a boat and tow the thing up there and get all the permits—it's never seemed worth it."

Healy's been fishing with two guides in particular for so long they've become more like most fishing buddies than anything else. "They are as much my friends as they are guides," he says. Tim Roller was at the tiller on that day of days. Healy has fished with Roller for more than a decade, and they were out on the Manistee River on Sep-tember 9, 2009, doing what the Rockford angler likes best—fishing for salmon.

"The best time—the real hit time—is that first hour or so in the morning just after daylight," Healy explains. Healy and Roller were out with Woodhouse, and the two clients had each landed a couple of salmon. After about an hour, Healy was getting in the groove, hoping for another "Healy Slam." That's what Roller calls a day in which the angler reels in a coho salmon, a chinook salmon, and a steelhead. Then he felt the hit. "I knew when I set the hook," he says. "I said, 'Wow, this is a good one!'"

A very good one. The fight lasted all of fifteen minutes—the brownie only attempted to jump once—before Healy was able to put the fish in the net and haul it aboard. "Only then did we realize one: how big this thing was, and two: it wasn't a salmon but a brown trout. Tim's eyes were bugging out."

They hefted the brownie onto the Boga Grip scale, and it proved too much for it, bottoming out at thirty pounds. Roller asked Healy how much he thought the fish weighed. He guessed about thirty-five. Roller got very excited. "Holy Cow," he said, "we could have a new record." They called another guide, Mark Chmura, who's

First introduced into North America in the late nineteenth century, brown trout have spread throughout a number of fisheries around the world, gradually becoming one of the most common and highly-prized of gamefish species.

something of a brown trout expert and just happened to be down-stream. Roller and Healy explained the situation.

"He said, 'Have you measured it? If it's over forty-one inches you've got a fish.' We measured it at forty-four inches, and he said, 'You may have a new record.'" Fifteen minutes later Chmura arrived with his pickup and a large cooler. "He looked at the fish and his eyes bugged out. These guys are doing an Indian War Hoop Dance," Healy recalls.

On the twenty-minute ride to downtown Manistee, Chmura turned to the others and said: "I'll call the DNR and the local news." They all showed up. Before long CNN arrived and Tim Roller was telling them: "Tom's put in his time. If anybody deserves this fish, Tom really deserves this fish."

•

"You'd think it was the Nobel Peace Prize," Roger Hellen said to the cameras as he displayed his record-breaking brown trout. The crowd roared. He and his fishing buddy Joe Miller were crammed into a tent at a fishing derby in Racine, Wisconsin. They'd just won the 2010 Salmon-A-Rama, bringing in the biggest fish ever recorded in the thirty-seven-year history of the competition, taking home a cool $10,700 for a few hours of fishing on Lake Michigan, and beating the Wisconsin state record in the process.

Roger Hellen's brown trout, as big as a log of firewood, weighed in at forty-one pounds eight ounces. Salmon-A-Rama official Cheryl Peterson, a Department of Natural Resources fisheries technician, told the local newspaper, "it was very exciting. It was certainly the biggest trout or salmon I've ever seen. We knew as soon as it was on the scale it was going to be a new state record."

A manager of Summit Packaging in Racine, Wisconsin, Roger Hellen's been fishing since he was in diapers in Kenosha, and he knew he had something big the moment he felt the bite. He and Miller had been out on Hellen's twenty-one-foot jet boat, *Get*

Hooked, since 4:30 a.m. that day. They'd waited for a couple of friends who never showed, so they got a later start than usual. They were off Wind Point in Lake Michigan and Hellen was trolling—a blue-green dolphin spoon on twenty-seven-pound test two-color lead-core line on planer boards, with fifteen feet of twenty-pound-test mono line as his leader. They'd been fishing an area about forty feet deep, and his line was about ten feet down, when he felt the strike. It was about eight o'clock.

"As soon as it hit we knew it was a sizable fish," he says. "And we knew from the way it was behaving that it was a brown trout."

And a fighter. The fish battled Hellen for three quarters of an hour. "We like to circle around the fish to get the line back and we went around it three times until we had about twenty yards of line out," he remembers. "Finally the line was almost straight up and down—we knew it was just underneath the boat—and the fish tired out. He made a dive for the bottom and within a minute we had him at the surface. We knew we really had something special."

Hellen had had some luck rolling dice just a few days before, winning seventy dollars. His luck held this morning. "We no more got him to the net and the hook popped out. If we had taken just a little bit longer he would have been gone."

They weighed the fish and their eyes grew wide as the needle pushed up over thirty-seven pounds, bouncing around in the forties. As they motored back to the marina, Hellen told his friend, Miller: "I bet we have a state record here. I was pretty certain." The bonus, of course, was that a fish of this size was almost certain to win the tournament, as well.

Even though he was sure he had a winner, Hellen went out again on the following Saturday, looking for something even bigger. He never found it. And nobody else did either. Hellen won the prize and the state record.

The world record was the next question.

●

It was Healy's guide who heard first. "Tim calls me and says, 'I understand a fellow caught a trout on the other side of the lake as big as yours.'" Healy joked: "I caught mine on this side of the lake, someone caught one on the other side of the lake—somebody ought to go out into the middle of the lake and catch a real big one." And it was true. The two fish were caught in the same watershed roughly 345 miles apart.

Tom Healy's brown weighed forty pounds seven ounces. Roger Hellen's was one ounce more. A single ounce. Roughly the weight of five quarters. Just enough to tip the scales in Hellen's favor. Tom Healy's world record, which he was able to enjoy for all of a year, goes to Roger Hellen, then, right?

Not according to the record keepers. The International Game Fish Association called the contest too close to call. Neck and neck. Nose to nose. A dead heat. According to IGFA's rules, a new record must surpass the old one by 0.5 percent. Which is more than two pounds in this case. So it's a tie.

Both men have been complete gentlemen about the situation. Healy admits he was "a little disappointed." But he's made no fuss, and he's happy that the records show how good fishing is in his area. "I don't want to challenge it," he says. "I respect everybody. Obviously, to have it IGFA certified he had to have it weighed and measured exactly."

As for Roger Hellen, he doesn't mind sharing, either. "I wasn't too concerned about whether it was world record or if it tied a world record. Not too many people pick up world-record books."

11

MUSKELLUNGE

CAL JOHNSON, FISHERMAN

On August 7, 1949, the *Milwaukee Sentinel* ran the headline, "Facts Prove Legality of Big Catch." The article that followed went on for several columns, shedding light on the world-record capture of a muskellunge taken in the waters of Lac Courte Oreilles, Wisconsin, a couple of weeks earlier.

"All of the facts without a single exception clearly and conclusively prove beyond the slightest shadow of a doubt," read the story, "that the world's record muskie taken by Cal Johnson in Lac Courte Oreilles on the morning of July 24 was legally caught, accurately weighed and measured, witnessed by reputable citizens and the papers were certified by notary John Morelan, well known member of the Wisconsin Conservation Commission, who inspected the fish personally."

Few fish have ever been so well documented. Weighed, measured, witnessed, weighed and measured again, then certified.

"Wisconsin" Cal Johnson was one of the nation's most famous outdoor writers when he pulled a 67.5-pound muskellunge out of Wisconsin's Lac Court Oreilles in 1949. Several muskie fisherman—a breed of their own—challenged the catch, and the controversy continues to this day. COURTESY OF THE IGFA

But some people weren't satisfied.

Almost as soon as Cal Johnson made his way back to shore at Lac Court Oreilles, a five-thousand-acre basin in north central Wisconsin, people were looking to find fault with the catch. This was muskie country, and any muskie claiming to be the biggest in the world was going to come under heavy scrutiny.

Even one caught by one of the most famous, upstanding muskie fishermen in the nation—"Wisconsin Cal."

●

Cal Johnson was born in Phillips, Wisconsin, in 1891, and began exploring the outdoors at an early age. According to legend, he hopped passing trains as a boy to get a ride to his favorite fishing holes. He enjoyed all kinds of sports—he played baseball, he wrestled competitively—but was always drawn back to the lakes and ponds of his home state.

After World War I, Johnson found work in a haberdashery, selling men's clothes. When that store failed, he started working in sporting goods. His love of the natural world prompted him to start writing, and he sold a story to the *Milwaukee Journal*. Home at night, he'd study the craft, and he kept at the typewriter. By 1926, the same newspaper was referring to him as "the famous outdoor writer." He'd sold many stories by then and rode a wave of notoriety and recognition that found him helping to set up fishing trips for Presidents Coolidge and Hoover.

In the late twenties, Johnson was the editor of *Outdoor America*, the magazine of the Isaak Walton League, one of the nation's earliest conservation organizations. His syndicated column was carried in hundreds of papers across the country. "Wisconsin Cal," as he came to be known, would go on to more glory in *Fishing Gamely for Game Fish* and *The Quest of the Bronze Back*, promotional fishing reels by the National Film Board of Canada, which were shown across the United States. The latter was filmed in Ontario in the late twenties and features Johnson camping beside Lake Weslemkoon and angling for smallmouth bass.

By the time Cal Johnson found himself on a fishing trip with his son, Phillip, and friend and fellow outdoor scribe Jack Conner in 1949, he'd been a fishing editor for both the *Minneapolis Tribune* and the *Chicago Daily News*, had served as the fishing editor of prestigious magazines such as *Outdoor Life* and *Sports Afield*, and helped establish the Outdoor Writers Association. His work had appeared in high-profile publications like *Esquire* and *Liberty* magazines, and he'd gained fame as a radio personality, hosting *Cal Johnson's Outdoor Lore* on NBC.

He'd penned countless articles—and reeled in even more muskies. One reference to Johnson in a 1969 edition of *Field & Stream* claimed he caught more than one thousand of the fish.

•

The muskellunge is one of those fish. Like the marlin and the largemouth, this "fish of ten thousand casts" has its own cult following. And in Wisconsin, where the relatively rare fish is commonly found, it's a prized trophy. The muskie was elected state fish in 1955, and the state Department of Natural Resources (DNR) estimates it has a population of about two hundred thousand.

The muskie is the biggest brother in the pike family and cousin to the pickerel. The unusual name is derived from an Ojibwa word translated through French, which means "ugly pike." The fish looks much like its kin, with an elongated body—it's about six times longer than it is deep—and spots and a dorsal fin set far back along its spine. Wisconsinites don't find it ugly at all.

Native to lakes great and big all across the upper Midwest and into Canada, muskellunge are particularly fond of Michigan, Minnesota, and the Badger State. They like clear water, preferably with some nice cover—rocks and reeds and grasses—and spend so much time in pond weeds that the big ones, as Cal Johnson pointed out in *Sports Afield*, are often called mossbacks for the green slime they collect on their topside. From their camouflaged position they set up ambushes for white suckers and other small fish, frogs, snakes, ducklings, mice, and even muskrats. (There's an old joke: A couple of muskie fishermen are doing their thing when they hear a woman screaming, "A huge fish just ate my dog. A fish just ate my dog." And the fishermen wander over and ask, "What color was your dog?")

Huge muskies in Wisconsin are tracked like trophy deer. This is a fish known for its massive size—typical muskies are in the two- to four-foot range, and weights between twenty and thirty pounds are not unusual. Cal Johnson once noted in *Sports Afield* that he'd found a six-pound walleye in the stomach of a muskie. Wisconsin has 700 some lakes and streams that are known to harbor muskellunge, and of these the majority are managed for large fish—those in excess of forty inches long—by the Wisconsin DNR.

They take their muskie very seriously in the Badger State—"Wisconsin offers some of the best muskellunge fishing on the planet," says a state-issued muskie fact sheet—and they proudly note that more world-record muskellunge have come out of their waters than any other.

The state of Wisconsin figures it takes the average muskie fisherman about fifty hours to catch a nice, legal, adult fish. That's according to their *Wisconsin Muskellunge Waters* booklet, which also points out that anglers after muskies tend to talk about "swirls," "follows," and "hits" as much or more than they do actual *catches*.

The fish is elusive. First you have to find one. The Wisconsin DNR estimates that for every two or three acres of muskie habitat there's one adult fish. Then if you can find one, and you can get it to bite, you have to be able to land it. Again, from Wisconsin DNR literature: "having one on the end of the line is the aquatic equivalent of having a tiger by the tail. . . . These famous fighters will drag the line underneath the boat or wrap it around the nearest submerged stump. They crack rods, strip reels, bend hooks, mutilate baits, and do whatever else they can to escape."

Which is why Wisconsin "muskie nuts" are so crazy about them. And why they're so protective of their world records.

•

Cal Johnson knew all this, of course. They didn't call him "Wisconsin Cal" for no good reason. He was a proud son of his home state, and when he got some bad news in the late 1940s, it was where he wanted to be. At a doctor's appointment, he was told that the rheumatic fever he'd had as a boy had weakened his heart, and that he only had a few months to live. That prompted the writer to leave his work and home in Minneapolis behind and move to the small "Quiet Lakes" town of Hayward, Wisconsin. And despite being cautioned by his physician that he should take it easy, he spent his days doing what he loved most—hunting and fishing—often in the company of his only child, Phillip.

That's what brought him to Lac Courte Oreilles on a summer weekend in July 1949. He and his son and his friend Jack Conner, outdoor editor of the *Minneapolis Star*, took rooms at the Moccasin Lodge on the shore of the lake, known for its muskellunge, about a fifteen-minute drive from his home. They'd spend the weekend fishing for muskie—looking for two particularly huge characters they'd encountered in previous visits but had been unable to land.

A thunderstorm blew in during Saturday night and was still rumbling around when the three anglers rolled out of bed in the wee hours of Sunday, the 24th. The clock read 3:30 a.m. Johnson liked to get going early, but he was daunted by the deluge pouring onto the roof of their cottage, and they waited a half hour before venturing outside.

When they hit the shore, Cal and Phil found the surface of the lake troubled by a southeast wind. Good. "To me, it looked like the ideal day for the big Musky to move around," Johnson wrote a couple of months later in an *Outdoors* magazine account of the catch. They launched one of the resort's sixteen-foot boats and began trolling about fifty feet out. The wooden rowboat was equipped with a 2.5 horsepower Champion motor, but the Johnsons preferred to row troll, and Phil was at the oars.

The rain slowed to a drizzle as Phil navigated the craft to a section of reeds, and Cal worked his lure. It was a small, chub-finished Pike Oreno at the end of thirty-pound Gladding line attached to a South Bend pole (just shy of five feet) on a South Bend Perfectereno reel. The water underneath was about fifteen feet deep, and Johnson let his lure wiggle at about six or eight feet.

Phil rowed; Cal trolled.

And then it hit. Hard.

Johnson felt "a terrific strike," causing a great adrenalin rush. Then the fish went quiet, and the fishermen puzzled over what he'd caught. "I thought for a moment that I had snagged a sturgeon in the nose for the fish did not move at first."

But the muskellunge began to do its "tell-tale back and forth movement" and Johnson understood what he had. "I realized we had hooked into one of the big Musky we had been fishing for during the past six weeks."

The writer prepared for a fight, yelling to Phil, "Son, I'm into one this time!" Cal began to coach his boy as to what he needed, but it really wasn't necessary, as Phil was a licensed guide himself and had spent many hours chasing muskies. He began to row out to deeper water. The fish didn't want to be led, forcing Johnson to let his line out. But eventually he came along, and the fisherman could feel "his great strength and weight."

Johnson decided to take the wisest course when sparring with an uncooperative fish and just sit tight. He knew if he attempted to haul in at this point, the weighty lunge would break either his line or his rod. "In handling any unusually large Musky," Johnson continued in his *Outdoors* piece, "it's wise to let the fish lead the battle."

So he waited it out.

The Johnsons kept the line taut and kept the fish fifty or sixty feet from the boat. As Phil recalled later: "We didn't want to get too close for fear he'd cut under the boat." They were patient and thankful for all the open water that surrounded their rowboat. "I think if this had been a flowage with many underwater trees we never would have gotten him."

Cal Johnson compared the action to hooking a large, ocean-going fish. "Big fish are not spectacular," he wrote. "They do not leap and swirl like smaller Musky. My record fish reminded me more of fishing for tuna. Actually, the fight was a grim tug-of-war with a giant that refused to show himself."

After a slow, grinding contest, Johnson decided to try and take the upper hand and began to pump the fish. The angler was surprised to find that the fish turned under the surface. He kept at it, leading the beast toward the boat. When the musky finally came up and turned on the surface, father and son got their first look. "When we actually saw his size we became a bit jittery and plenty excited. And who wouldn't?"

Phil was struck by how massive the creature was. "This fish actually came as no surprise to us because we figured it was the same fish we raised three or four times earlier that season. One time it followed within six feet of the boat and made a vicious strike at the lure. It was the biggest fish we'd ever seen!"

They figured there was no way they were hauling this one over their gunwales, so Cal asked Phil to row to shore and beach it. "The next ten minutes gave my heart the greatest strain it will ever endure," the elder Johnson wrote. But he stayed tough and they finally got close enough to shore for Phil to jump overboard with the gaff. "It's difficult for me to recall what happened next," Johnson explained in his magazine piece, "but there stood Phil on the shore beside the fish, its glistening body looking like something that weighed all of one hundred pounds. I wilted in the boat and

I know that my son, who is twenty-three years old, was a nervous wreck, for he was pale and trembling."

But the battle was won.

They hefted the fish into the boat and sparked the motor, speeding back to the dock. When they got there, "bedlam broke loose," Cal recalled. "The owners and guests of the lodge came running in their pajamas, like volunteer firemen in a small town."

It was barely six o'clock.

When they arrived on shore, Cal and Phil met back up with Conner, who had taken out his own boat. They took the fish to a scale in Moccasin Lodge's garage and were shocked by what they read—seventy-seven pounds. "Don't get too excited," the owner told them. "That includes these boards and a gunnysack." When the scale was cleaned off and the fish was weighed properly, they were still stunned.

Sixty-seven and a half pounds.

A new world record.

They took some photos and then decided to bring the fish to Hayward's local taxidermist, Karl Kahmann, to be weighed again on a certified scale, measured with a steel tape, and preserved for posterity.

"Wisconsin Cal" Johnson, outdoor celebrity, had just become "Wisconsin Cal" Johnson, world-record muskie fisherman. He'd spend his last years speaking, visiting groups, and presiding at sportsmen's shows, before a heart attack took him in 1953. He was sixty-two.

His world record stands to this day.

●

That is, according to some. The International Game Fish Association considers the Lac Courte Oreilles muskellunge to be the world's largest. The State of Wisconsin and the National Freshwater Fishing Hall of Fame, right there in Hayward, however, consider the biggest muskie ever caught to be the one taken by Louis Spray just three months after Johnson, again right there in Hayward at Chippewa Flowage. Spray's muskie weighed in at sixty-nine pounds eleven ounces. If you ask the World Record Muskie Alliance (WRMA), an organization founded in 2006 because its members were disgusted with the records held by officialdom, another muskie altogether is the champion.

The waters truly get murky when it comes to muskie. The people of Wisconsin take this all very seriously. There are conspiracy theories that rival those involving certain presidential assassinations and the falling of the twin towers.

First the Louis Spray story. Before Cal Johnson retired to Hayward, Louis Spray was the local fishing legend. He kept a bar in town and was reputed to have been a smuggler during the Prohibition era. But could he fish, landing not one but two world record muskies—a fifty-nine-and-a-half-pounder in 1939 and a sixty-one-pound–thirteen-ounce giant a year later. Word goes that when Johnson beat his record, Spray "came out of retirement" to catch an even bigger fish. That's when he caught "Chin-Whiskered Charlie." He spent nineteen straight days slow-trolling in an area of the Chippewa Flowage, a river created when the Chippewa River was dammed in 1923. He'd seen a monster muskellunge there, and he wanted him. After weeks he finally got him, and, upon doing so, he shot Chin-Whiskered Charlie in the face with a .22 handgun, a practice that was not uncommon.

IGFA was not impressed. Firearms are not allowed in its world records.

So Cal Johnson remained king of the world. Spray, however, became the big man in Hayward, Wisconsin—until 1957, when Art Lawton of Albany, New York, reeled in a sixty-nine-pound–fifteen-ounce muskie in the St. Lawrence River. But IGFA didn't like his fish either, determining that it couldn't have been as big as he said, upon examination of photographic evidence. So they stuck with Cal Johnson and everyone else stuck with Louis Spray.

So the story goes.

According to the World Record Muskie Alliance, it wasn't all quite so simple.

Jerry Newman, the organization's founder, believes in a darker version of the tale, which begins with Louis Spray and Cal Johnson meeting at the bar. "[T]he short story goes that Louie revealed the details on how he faked his two previous world records," he says. When Johnson went out and did same, Spray was ". . . pissed. Word on the street was that Louie would pay top dollar for another big muskie and shortly thereafter Spray registered his third world record, which just happened to beat Cal by just a couple of pounds."

Newman believes Cal Johnson's story was ultimately "pure fiction." And that the fisherman himself was "probably a pretty decent guy who just decided to take advantage of a soft spot in the sport-fishing industry." According to Newman, the outdoor writer figured out a "foolproof way to beat the system and get a new car, several endorsements, and of course elevate his personal fame." (They claim that Spray made more than three thousand dollars after his first catch—a sum that would be twenty-thousand-something in today's dollars.)

In June of 2008, the WRMA submitted to IGFA a thirty-four-page report discounting Cal Johnson's muskie. The document essentially says that Johnson's fish was neither as long nor as girthy as the photographs make it appear, and that it was extended and fleshed out when mounted. And, it goes on, the photographs prove it. The report has several contributions from specialists in photographic forensics and from attorneys who gave their imprimatur to the findings.

The IGFA wasn't buying. The association's conservation director wrote to the WRMA that their "report was vetted at the highest possible level at IGFA" but "we simply do not feel that the photogrammetry analysis is sufficient for us to rescind this record."

This, of course, didn't sit well with Newman. WRMA "obviously uncovered a lot more than what's in the summary report," he says. Newman has "no faith" in IGFA and thinks senior members "probably realize that many of their other records are fakes too, but still elect to sit on their hands." Why? "Because they are in the business of promoting and selling fishing records, and the disqualification of a cornerstone record like Cal's is simply bad for business."

The WRMA recognizes yet another fish—the fifty-eight-pounder caught in 2009 by Joe Seeberger in Wisconsin's Elk River Chain of Lakes.

•

Skepticism met Cal Johnson's muskie as soon as it came ashore. In the weeks following the catch, many questions were asked in the pages of the newspaper. Some claimed the fish was dead when he found it. Some were bothered by a mix-up regarding whether Jack Conner was in the boat when the fish was caught. That's how it came across when Cal and Phil Johnson and Conners came walking up with the monster muskie that morning, and none of them did anything to dispel the notion. (Others even claimed Conner actually reeled in the fish himself.) Some thought the fish had probably been speared, which would disqualify it.

The *Milwaukee Sentinel* finally came to Johnson's defense with its August 7 story, calling him "a man of national reputation" whose "writings over the years portray his character better than anything we can say about him." It was a long piece that strove to answer all the questions and put the whole affair to bed. They interviewed witnesses and talked at length to Karl Kahmann, the taxidermist, bearer of a "most enviable reputation" who had stuffed over five thousand muskies by that time. He insisted that the fish was fresh when it came to him, bore no evidence of trapping, spearing, or netting, showed hook marks in the jaw—and was every bit as big as Johnson claimed.

"Karl further stated," the paper continued, "that the weights were double checked and that the two scales gave exactly the same reading . . . 67 pounds 8 ounces. . . . Measurements, he said, were taken with a steel tape.

"Karl Kahmann's statements definitely eliminate all possibility that the fish might have been speared, netted or trapped," the paper argued. "The fish didn't die of disease or old age. It did not carry so much as a bullet mark because the fish was gaffed. The fish was still limp when weighed and measured. With all this evidence clear and above board, just where we ask, CAN there be any deception?"

More than fifty years later and people are still wondering.

12

HAMMERHEAD SHARK

BUCKY DENNIS, FISHERMAN

"Selfish miscreant."

"Ignorant Inbreed."

"Cancer of the earth."

"Moron."

"Absolute waste of life."

Everyone, it seems, has an opinion on Clyde "Bucky" Dennis. The Tampa Bay fisherman has been called a lot of things since he landed the hammerhead shark that won him a world record. While most of the fishermen who join him in the record books have been celebrated for their catches and enjoy life as outdoor celebrities—having their pictures taken with fans, signing sponsorship deals, doing interviews and appearances—Dennis has spent several years defending himself.

Bucky Dennis (left) caught two giant, world-record hammerhead sharks in Florida's Boca Grande Pass—and launched a tidal wave of controversy when it was revealed that both sharks were pregnant. COURTESY OF THE IGFA

"They called me a redneck who wants to kill things—all kinds of stuff," he says, referring to the countless people who posted their thoughts about him in online forums. These online pundits number in the thousands. The *Los Angeles Times* ran a piece in May of 2009 entitled, "Giant Hammerhead Shark Catch: Is Florida Angler Hero or Villain?" That same month an article about the catch on the website of his local *Tampa Bay Times* generated almost four hundred comments, the vast majority of them negative.

Dennis takes it all very philosophically. "They don't know me," he says, with a surprising lack of malice. "Anybody who's ever fished with me has a totally different view of who I am and how I act. These people sit behind a desk at their computer and put their comments out there. . . . I suppose it's a free country."

Much of the tidal wave of controversy came because people simply don't like shark fishing. It resonates with many the way that whale hunting does—an unnecessary killing of a majestic sea creature—only with a bit more edge. Sharks, of course, are dangerous and endangered. Florida passed a law banning the killing of hammerheads, which went into effect on January 1, 2012, so dispatching them is seen not only as wrong but as mean-spirited and vengeful. (Like Bucky Dennis, TV icon Rosie O'Donnell attracted the ire of thousands of tweeters and bloggers for taking her family out on several hammerhead hunting expeditions in the past few years.) Attitudes have changed a lot since the days of Peter Benchley's *Jaws*.

In the case of this one-thousand-pound hammerhead, though, there was more to the outcry. The shark was caught in Tampa Bay's Boca Grande Pass in May. At that time of year there's a reason some sharks grow large—they're pregnant. The likelihood that the shark was pregnant was so great that Robert Hueter, Director of the Shark Research Center at Mote Marine Laboratory in Sarasota, turned down Dennis's donation of the body from simply looking at photos and videos. "I just didn't want to accept that specimen and encourage the killing of pregnant females," he told the *Tampa Bay Times*, noting that the population of hammerheads is down 75 to 90 percent in the Gulf of Mexico alone.

Dennis understands all these arguments. "Some people want to save the world," he told the *Tampa Bay Times*.

"But they don't know me."

•

The response to the catch was nothing new for the thirty-nine-year-old angler. Bucky Dennis had been through these waters before. In 2006, he caught his first world-record hammerhead. A guide by profession, he was working out in Boca Grande Pass on a busy, early May day. That's the time of year to stalk sharks off the west coast of Florida.

"In April, sharks come because they're waiting for the tarpon," Dennis explains. "They'll come for the blood. They'll come right to me." As spring settles across Tampa Bay, the fishing becomes more difficult. "In later May it gets harder to catch sharks because all they want to do is eat tarpon. It's hard to get them to go for your bait."

On May 23, Dennis had his work cut out for him. Dinner was on for the hammerheads. From April to August, giant silver king tarpon migrate up into Boca Grande Pass to feed and spawn, giving the region the largest populations of tarpon in the world. The pass is the "big mouth" at the southern tip of Gasparilla Island, and its waters are notoriously deep and rich with life.

And the fish were about in abundance—if the number of boats full of eager fishermen were any indication. "There were a hundred boats out there fishing for tarpon that day," Dennis recalls.

The guide had already hooked a massive bull shark on this particular Thursday, a fish that he wrestled with for quite some time—and a fish that he wanted. But his line got crossed with a tarpon fisherman's, and the man's wife cut Dennis's line.

"I was really, really angry," he remembers. Frustrated, he loaded his rod for one more go, putting the last bait of the day on his one-hundred-pound PowerPro line: a fish that hammerheads consider an even bigger treat than tarpon—a twenty-pound stingray. It was 11:30 a.m.

Looking out across the waters of the Boca Grande, he could see some tarpon guides doing donuts with their boats, like frat boys on JetSkis. He knew what it meant. "Other fishermen will do circles in their boat to scare off the sharks," he says. "They don't want them eating their tarpon." He turned his twenty-three-foot flats skiff in that direction, and before long, he caught a glimpse of her.

"I could see the shark," he remembers. "I saw her fin and she had two bull sharks on her tail." The bulls follow the hammerheads around like little brothers follow big brothers. "The hammerhead is king. They have jurisdiction. The bull won't touch tarpon until the hammerhead hits it."

Dennis moved into striking distance and dropped the stingray overboard. Within minutes, he felt a strong hit, and he pulled up to set the hook. But he wasn't sure which of the fish had taken the bait.

"I didn't know if I had one of the bull sharks," he says. Then the shark turned and started to swim perpendicularly out from shore, and he began to get excited. "That's a characteristic of a hammerhead. I don't know why, but it's like they take a bearing and swim off in a straight line toward it. I knew I had the big hammerhead."

Dennis was able to get a message to a fishing buddy on one of the tarpon boats—he was going to need help to land this one. His friend Brian Hart hopped aboard and took the wheel, maneuvering around the armada of fishing boats, allowing Dennis to sit in the fighting chair and concentrate on landing his leviathan. Once out past all the tarpon boats, a few of Dennis's other guide friends climbed aboard to help.

He'd been fishing close enough to shore to see the swimmers on the beach, and now his boat was slowly being pulled out to sea. "It was an eerie feeling. You're getting dragged offshore by a monster shark." Shallow, flat vessels, skiffs like the twenty-three-foot one he was piloting begin to seem very small when fighting fourteen-foot sharks, and problems tend to magnify the further you get from shore. "I looked back, and I couldn't see land anymore," the fisher-man remembers. "After a while your cell phone doesn't work any-more." They were all alone in a wilderness of water attached to a massive man-eater.

The hammerhead hauled Dennis's boat twelve miles out before doing a one-eighty and pulling him back toward shore. Then she twisted again and started for deep water a second time. By now, the fisherman's back hurt, and his legs ached. And she'd only just begun to fight. "Of course, it's one thing hooking them up and another thing to get them to the boat," Dennis notes. "It's a big animal—and dangerous."

Fierce fighters, hammerheads will gladly bring the battle to the boat. Once considered the third-most dangerous shark species by the US Navy—behind the great white and tiger sharks—the species are notoriously difficult to land.

"When you grab the leader, it's always tricky," says Dennis. "The fish will swing its head back and forth—a four- or five-foot swing—and it's pulled my shoulder almost out of the socket a couple of times."

Hammerheads are famous for their endurance. "I've had a big bull shark, four hundred pounds or more, and I've gotten it to the boat, had it tagged and measured—all in fifteen minutes. I've gotten pretty efficient. But a hammerhead will fight for hours."

Five in this case. It took more than ten tries for Dennis's friend to get a gaff hook into the fish and for the guide to be able to grab the leader. When the shark felt the hook pierce her dorsal fin she really started to thrash and fought for more than a half hour before finally settling to her fate. When she let up, they were able to get a second gaff in behind the gills, and lasso her with the all important tail rope. After that she was done.

Hammerhead sharks are typically found along coastlines and continental shelves in warmer waters. As opposed to certain other species of large sharks, hammerheads will often be seen in schools.

When the battle was finally over, the weary fisherman had her tied up head and tail and turned for the long journey home. "Now we have to go all the way back to the Gasparilla Marina. That's something like twenty miles away now, and we were just poking along."

Dennis thought if they could pull part of the shark up onto the stern, it would allow them to go faster. He and three of his buddies dragged for all they were worth, but they only managed to get the hammerhead up onto the rear deck. "That didn't work at all," remembers Dennis—the aft half of the small boat started going under. A tow it would be.

By the time they got to the marina a crowd was waiting. "There were a hundred people on the dock. The announcer from the professional tarpon show was there with his camera and microphone. It was a big deal when we got back. Pretty neat. By the end of the day I was wore out."

●

Bucky Dennis came out of the womb a competitor. The Dennis family lived on the south side of St. Petersburg, on the shores of Tampa Bay, and when he wasn't playing soccer or football—he was a natural athlete—the young Bucky could be found fishing. "Since I was old enough to hold a pole," he says. "I'd wade fish, jig fish, catch flounder and trout—whatever I could. I love to eat fish."

Which was ideal, as his father is a fish biologist who worked for the state of Florida, specializing in snook, an extremely popular sport species in the area. While working for the Department of Marine Resources, the senior Dennis studied snook and redfish reproduction, growing the small fish for stocking projects, and writing a book about his findings. "He was the first one to reproduce them in captivity," says his son, proudly.

As soon as he was old enough to drive, Bucky was using his father's boat on fishing trips and—no real surprise—he developed a love for fishing snook. But it didn't matter what he was after, it was the sport that he thrived upon. (He took that same enthusiasm to the woods as well. "In winter we'd go up north to visit family in Alabama and hunt for deer," he says.)

He was always driven internally, always wanted to win. In high school he was a wrestler. Then it was dirt-bike racing. "That's part of my problem," he explains. "I was competitive all the way up. I wanted to catch the biggest fish. I wanted to beat the other guys wrestling. I did a bit of motocross—until I had a couple of crashes. I want to beat everyone at snook tournaments."

After high school he took a job welding towers onto boats. And after a while he discovered that people would pay for the fishing expertise that he'd picked up as a kid. "I got my guide's license in ninety-eight, and I've guided ever since then." Business got good several years ago. "Once you get a record," he says, "you get a clientele."

Now he can provide for his family—wife, two boys, two girls—working a single financial quarter. "I work really hard for three months of the year at one hundred dollars an hour. April, May, June." He guides for sharks, of course, but also for tarpon and grouper.

During his off time he finds he needs to feed his inner competitor. He likes to gamble. To watch football. "I like to play Texas Hold 'em. Some days off I'll go to the dog track in Bonita Springs or Sarasota."

But most of all, he likes to fish. "I fish most days of the year. As my boys get older I spend a lot of time showing them all of my tricks. If I can keep them from fighting. They're very competitive. They both wrestle too, and the younger one does mixed martial arts. He thinks he's going to be an MMA star."

In summer he'll often take the boys out for giant snook. "Everything that's big," Dennis says simply, "I like to catch."

•

Bucky Dennis and his buddy drove the hammerhead out to a state-certified truck weigh station, the only scale large enough, and once they got their trailer parked they were ecstatic—the shark weighed 1,280 pounds, beating the previous record by almost three hundred pounds. Dennis made sure he had everything needed to document his catch.

"Then I was sitting there with a big shark, thinking, 'what am I going to do with this thing?' My buddy suggested we call up Mote Marine Laboratory, and we donated it." Which made perfect sense to the son of a marine biologist. That first hammerhead they accepted.

The lab said in a statement: "Mote scientists discovered that the shark was pregnant with 55 pups, including 52 near full term and three that were underdeveloped. Experts previously believed that great hammerheads gave birth to 20-40 pups at a time. ("I guess she was a whore," Dennis says. "She'd been sleeping around too much.")

"Mote scientists were also able to examine and weigh the shark's organs," the statement continued, "and examine the food in its stomach—the rear half of a 5-foot tarpon, tarpon scales and a southern stingray believed to be the fisherman's bait—supporting our understanding of great hammerhead biology and feeding."

Mote froze the shark and made a mold of it, creating six full-size, fiberglass copies, which were distributed to Bass Pro Shops. "They have a mold hung up in all their shops," Dennis says.

She was an impressive specimen and made a fine model. As soon as the story of the catch appeared in the papers, though, the comments started to fly.

"Not one person came up to me or gave me a hard time. Around here people congratulated me," Dennis recalls. "It was people online saying really mean, nasty stuff."

Meanwhile, Dennis kept looking for an even bigger hammerhead.

•

Television icon Rosie O'Donnell can empathize with Bucky Dennis. She found herself in a similar situation in early 2012 after a photo of her standing next to a huge, bloody hammerhead hanging from a hook surfaced on the web. O'Donnell has a home in Miami and had taken her family shark fishing with Miami Beach guide Mark "the Shark" Quartiano several times before the taking of three species of hammerhead was outlawed by the state of Florida on January 1 of that year.

The snapshot caused a huge outcry—an explosion of criticism on O'Donnell's Twitter feed—and she was forced to defend herself on her show, claiming she was a "friend to all animals."

As all of this was happening, conservation biologist Samantha Whitcraft reached out to O'Donnell, offering to show her the inside of a shark lab, but the TV personality failed to take her up on it. Whitcraft works for Shark Savers, an organization dedicated to the preservation of hammerheads and other sharks.

"We worked very hard to make sure all three species of hammerheads in Florida waters are protected," she says. "If you look at the anecdotal evidence, divers used to see hammerheads on a regular basis, and now it's very rare. Back when Bucky Dennis was landing his world-record hammerheads, you can be sure the populations were depressed."

A new study from the *Marine Policy* journal bears this out, quantifying for the first time the annual damage done to shark species worldwide. The peer-reviewed report released in March of 2013 states that about one hundred million sharks were killed in 2010, most of them by commercial fishermen. The fish are dying at a rate that "exceeds their ability to recover." In other words, it's unsustainable, and the populations of sharks everywhere are becoming threatened.

Shark species tend to reproduce more slowly than other animals, taking longer to grow and mature and producing fewer offspring that survive. Which is why Samantha Whitcraft was so offended that Dennis's catch was pregnant.

"That's just horrendous," she says. "In fishing there's no regard for the individual animal. If that had been a pregnant elephant or tiger or bear—an animal we humans relate to—they'd be storming down his door."

The Mote Marine Laboratory wasn't impressed, telling Bucky Dennis they didn't want his second shark, citing in a statement:

"We declined to accept another large hammerhead in favor of promoting catch-and-release fishing—a choice that we have long encouraged for our nation's recreational shark fisheries. Mote tracks released sharks with satellite transmitters and other kinds of tags, gaining exciting new knowledge about shark habitat use and ecology, potentially revealing vital places where they mate and give birth. This kind of research also allows scientists and anglers to work together. Mote scientists tag sharks caught by anglers in a new annual catch-and-release, conservation-focused tournament (begun in 2010) called the Guy Harvey Ultimate Shark Challenge. Capt. Dennis has participated in this tournament and recently declared that he supports this catch-and-release model and enjoys contributing to shark research."

•

Because of all the outcry, Bucky Dennis won't be catching any more hammerheads.

"I'm done with the record thing for now. Unless IGFA would let me catch a twenty-foot hammerhead and measure the length, get the girth, and film and document it. But I'm not going to kill another one. I've had enough problems."

These days, the Florida fisherman is continuing to guide aspiring anglers, and he's working with the Guy Harvey Ultimate Shark Challenge, an annual tournament based in nearby Punta

Gorda, which bills itself as the "next generation" of shark-fishing competitions—it's based on not only sport but science and conservation as well. No kills are allowed and points are deducted if an animal is even handled inappropriately.

"I am behind them 100 percent," Dennis told *Waterline* magazine in the spring of 2011. "I can see what they're doing, I'm into the research with it—I help Mote whenever I get a chance now."

He's become fascinated with the science behind the hammerhead and wants to know more about his former adversary. "I want to see where they go," he continued. "I want to see where they migrate to. I love the hammerhead, even though I do have the record. Some people might not see it that way, but that's the way it is."

With the Guy Harvey Challenge, Dennis is using the decades of experience he's amassed to show anglers not the best ways to take big sharks but how to safely catch and release the powerful creatures.

Not only is it the right thing to do, he says, but the state of Florida has made it illegal to catch hammerheads anyway. Which works out well for record holders. "If you could get the rest of the world to follow—that'd be great," Dennis says.

"I'd have the world record forever."

PACIFIC BLUE MARLIN
STACEY PARKERSON, FISHERWOMAN

Stacey Parkerson's high school girlfriends don't quite know what to make of her now. And the vivacious, outgoing native of Evergreen, Colorado, is amazed at the turns her life has taken too. "My friends laugh," she says. "I was captain of the cheerleading squad, just a typical girlie girl. I never imagined I'd be a champion fishing woman."

But that's exactly where the thirty-three-year-old finds herself today. Parkerson's a self-described "professional angler" who spends almost half the year cruising the waters off Costa Rica, Mexico, Venezuela, Panama, the Dominican Republic, and several other Caribbean islands in search of world records to break.

So far she's felled fifty-three of them and won almost enough trophies and honors to fill her custom, fifty-two-foot Paul Spencer

Two-time IGFA's Lady Angler of the Year, Stacey Parkerson poses with a black marlin caught by her coach Enrico Capozzi at IGFA's headquarters. Parkerson has caught more than fifty world records.
COURTESY OF STACEY PARKERSON AND ENRICO CAPOZZI

boat. The list is extraordinary: IGFA World Record Achievement Award in 2009 for most saltwater world records by a woman. Two-time Top 10 IGFA Lady Angler of the Year for most world records. Three-time Billfish Foundation Lady Angler of the Year for most billfish tagged and released. First lady angler in angling history to achieve a Fantasy Slam of billfish world records with five species. First woman in the annals to catch a white marlin world record on twelve- and eight- and six-pound tippet fly rods. First lady angler to land Atlantic sailfish world records on four-, six-, and eight-pound tippet. That's just the bill of the fish—the list goes on and on.

All because she met an Italian fashion maven in 2000 who saw something in her.

"She's done phenomenally well," says that man, Parkerson's mentor, boyfriend, best friend, and fishing coach, Enrico Capozzi, who himself holds fifty-six world fishing records. "In any competitive sport there's a lot of training that goes into trying to be the best. In tennis, say, some people spend years training and training, but in the end there is one that is better than the others. There's a gift—an intuition, a coordination in your movements and sight—that makes someone that much better. Stacey was lucky enough to have crossed paths with her gift."

●

The seeds were always there. Girlie girl though she may have been, Parkerson had worked a fishing pole long before she met Enrico Capozzi. Her father was a special agent in the FBI, and she spent four years in the Rocky Mountain town of Evergreen, Colorado, before he was transferred to a narcotics unit in Miami in 1983. There, the young Parkerson was quickly smitten. "My parents exposed me to the outdoors, I loved to hike and camp, and growing up in Florida I always loved the ocean," she says.

Fishing came early—and she relished the challenge. "I had a Snoopy rod as a child," she says, "and I fished with my little brother behind our house in Coral Springs, Florida, in the C14 canal." Even then she was interested in records—the outfish-your-brother bragging-rights prize. "I was always very competitive with him, trying to cast farther and catch more fish."

The Parkerson family had a farm in Eastman, Georgia, and she fished the pond there as well, and she'd also occasionally dig out a pole and drop lines over the rails of the pontoon boat when she went to visit grandparents in Waconia, Minnesota, in summers. But it wasn't until she met Enrico Capozzi in Key West that she started to get really serious about the sport. Before that her interests ran to competitive cheerleading and dance. "Girlie girl stuff," as she puts it. Her world was suddenly turned on its head.

"I met Enrico, and we dated for two months before he invited me on a trip to Costa Rica," she says. "He was targeting a blue marlin world record." The fisherman made the catch and the excitement and drama of the contest made a profound impact on the girl from Florida.

"I was beyond excited to learn and try for myself," she says. "I was shaking, and even cried a bit. . . . We had such an amazing time that we hired the captain, bought a boat, and started our new chapter of life and love in Costa Rica."

Capozzi remembers the day. "I was lucky enough to land a world record," he says. "A very important world record. And she was there, and I could see it in her face. I thought to myself, 'We may have someone who's into this.'"

Parkerson was soon in the fighting chair herself—and into it she was. "She caught a Pacific sailfish, and she had tears in her eyes from the excitement," Capozzi says.

●

Traveling the world in search of adventure is something Enrico Capozzi inherited from his father. Born in Milan, the fifty-year-old angler lived in Italy until he turned sixteen, but he spent a lot of time globetrotting with his dad. One particular trip took them on safari in Africa, hunting. "My father had a friend who was into fishing and one day in Africa we decided to go off the Indian Coast," Capozzi says. They went in search of big billfish, and they found some. The friend got a bite, but it was the young Capozzi who was struck. "I watched him catch a marlin, and it touched something inside me, and it sort of propelled me in my life. I wrapped my life around it."

The aspiring angler took several fishing trips with his father after that, chasing billfish across the seven seas—"Africa, Mexico, Panama, and on and on," he says. When a job opportunity called to him from the Caribbean, he jumped. "My family had business interests there, and I moved there when I was sixteen." For a young kid captivated by marlin and swordfish and sailfish, it was idyllic. "I was basically catapulted to the tropics with strategic access to some fantastic places—some of the best billfishing in the world."

Capozzi spent several decades working for his family in the fashion industry and fishing as often as he could. When he retired in 1989, he "completely dedicated his life to it."

In November of 2000, he'd meet Parkerson, his competitive counterpart, who would dedicate her life to it too. "He invited me on a sailing trip in the Caribbean for two weeks in January, 2001," she recalls. "That trip we truly hit it off and, to make a long story short, I never returned home."

Instead, she began what she calls the "*Spirit of Pilar* Fishing School," a deep immersion in deepwater fishing she was put through by Capozzi and his *Spirit of Pilar* crew. (The boat was christened such in homage to Hemingway's famous thirty-eight-foot fishing vessel, *Pilar*.)

"You do not catch records right away," Parkerson is quick to point out. The rudiments come first. The young angler began by learning to hook and fight the fish. When she had a handle on those skills she moved on to learning to control and turn the fish.

"From there I learned to catch sailfish from a dead boat in less than three minutes," she explains, "like they do at the Masters tournament, which," she points out, "still doesn't allow woman anglers." While this was going on, Capozzi was targeting a sailfish world record on two-pound line. Whenever the fish looked like it was smaller than the one-hundred-pounders he was after, Stacey would work it instead. "We were heavy into catch and release, tagging all our catches for the Billfish Foundation."

•

Cruising the coastline of Costa Rica, spending days fishing in the sun sounds idyllic, but being a novice and the only woman on a boat of experienced men made it difficult going for the former cheerleader. "A lot of emotion would get involved on my part," she says. "I'm all woman all the time—on one hand I am a girlie girl—but I wanted to be treated as an equal, so it's a balancing act."

"Training wasn't easy," Capozzi says simply.

Parkerson pushed on, and in September of 2003 she was rewarded with her first world record, a horse-eye jack on six-pound line. "It was a small fish, but for me a proud moment. I was gaining respect from the crew."

Winning the approval of the captain and her shipmates was crucial for Parkerson. "It's a team sport for us 1,000 percent. We've always had our own personal crew. If one guy is off for a day we're all off."

The young angler was eager to put that new-found respect to work and land more records. She and Capozzi spent a good deal of time in Golfito, a small Costa Rican port near Panama, once

Stacey Parkerson with the 187-pound–4-ounce world-record blue marlin she caught in 2007. COURTESY OF STACEY PARKERSON

headquarters of the notorious United Fruit Company. Among the wettest places on earth—averaging more than two hundred inches of rain annually—it's very close to inshore waters brimming with mullet snapper.

When Parkerson and Capozzi were there, IGFA added the fish to its books. "It was a perfect opportunity for Enrico to teach me the different line classes and to have fun catching world records," she says. Between them, Parkerson and Capozzi won every line class for both men and woman for mullet snapper. "It was a wonderful learning curve, and it taught me so much about knowing my abilities, how much pressure I could use, and above all the knowledge of playing a fish on all line classes. It took many trips, and we caught many records until it was time to target the ultimate arena of billfish records!"

•

The big one for Stacey Parkerson came as a Christmas present in December of 2007. Of all her records, her dance with the "lady in the blue dress" is the one she looks back on most fondly. "I'm particularly proud of being the first woman in history to catch a world-record blue marlin," she says.

She and Capozzi and their crew of three were tracking billfish off the coast of Costa Rica. The Pacific coast of the Central American nation is about the middle of the range of the Pacific blue marlin, which stretches from southern California to Chile. The Pacific and Atlantic blue marlins are virtually identical, and biologists continue to debate exactly how closely they're related.

The fish migrate for miles—they're the most tropical in the marlin family, preferring the equatorial ocean—but the waters off Costa Rica are known to be a year-round haven. Famous for their spearlike bills, tall crowns, and huge tails, they're the largest of their marlin brothers and sisters, typically reaching lengths of eleven feet or more and weights upwards of one thousand pounds. At the upper end of the food chain, the striped beasts feed on tuna and squid and mackerel and are themselves considered a delicacy by great whites.

Parkerson found hers in calm seas off Playa Carrillo on a beautiful day. It was the week before Christmas, and she was geared out and ready. "The rods are special blanks and the fly reels are made by Abel and modified for my hand," she says. The line was sixteen-pound Stren, and at the end of her line was an "Enrico Special," a custom fly tied by Capozzi.

She and her crew had spotted the fish and she cast out to it. The marlin showed a bit of interest and then turned away. "He kept coming back," she remembers. "It took me about seven or eight casts till I got a good bite on a fly."

When he did bite, he ran, which blue marlin are wont to do. The big billfish are notoriously quick sprinters, hitting speeds up to sixty miles per hour. Parkerson's reel began to spin violently. "It's the fastest I ever had line coming off my fly reel ever." Not only did he sprint away, but he dove and disappeared.

"It was a difficult fish, and he stayed on the bottom for a long time," she says. The angler's problems mounted. Commercial fishermen frequently longline for billfish in Costa Rica, creating vast tentacles of cable and line. These pelagic arrays are typically set up near the surface and may have as many as one thousand hooks attached, and they pose problems for not only sport fishermen but also for sea turtles and many species of marlin and swordfish.

Conservationists have been after governments to place limits on these rigs. Says Ellen Peel of the Billfish Foundation: "One of the primary issues we're facing with billfish conservation in Costa Rica," she told the press, "is that medium-sized commercial long-line fishing operations primarily target mahi mahi and tuna and can fish within the first forty miles from shore. In this area, incidental catches of sailfish can be a big problem."

And there are other concerns, as Stacey Parkerson found—a long line lay in between her and her world-record fish. "I had to back off on the line and we had to get it cut," she says. "We would never have done that in our conventional fishing, but we knew this was a serious potential record." Once past this line, she tripped again. "I got back on him real good and sure enough we came across another long line."

As the clock spun, the difficulties mounted, and they weren't all external. Exhausted, Parkerson was battling her own mental toughness. "The hard part is the first two hours—it's a battle between your mind and your body," she says. "Once I hit the two-hour mark I get into a Zenlike state and it gets easier."

Another hour on, though, and she felt herself breaking down. "Once I got to the three- to four-hour mark I was really hurting." But she knew what she had and she wasn't letting it get away. "For the last hour we could see him the entire time twenty feet down."

The feisty marlin dragged the boat all over. "We traveled somewhere between seventeen and twenty miles with this fish." But Parkerson was able to overcome both herself and the strong marlin. "We kept a particular angle and we were able to bring the fish up slowly but surely."

And then he was at the boat. Crew members ran to get their hooks. First one, then two, then three went over the side. "Everyone had a gaff in him," she recalls. "It was intense. *Intense.*"

"My goodness what a battle that was," Capozzi says. "It gives me goose bumps to think about it."

Parkerson found herself overwhelmed when the 187-pound–4-ounce marlin made it into the hold. The fish was huge—seven feet long, forty-four-inch waist—and she knew she had another record in the bag. It was the thirty-fourth world beater that she'd caught, and yet it still struck her in a profound way. "Once we got the fish in it was a huge emotional release for me. I sat on the edge of the cockpit and cried my eyes out."

•

As someone interested in billfish—in 2010 he became the first angler to release ten thousand of them—Capozzi says it's not really worth trying to go for all-tackle records anymore. The fish simply aren't there. "If you look at the world records for billfish, they're very old," he says. "There's a reason for that."

When he was younger, Capozzi spent more than a decade chasing the Pacific sailfish world record for the two-pound line, which was a fish of 111 pounds. He went at it full force, cruising the seas with his crack team. "I fished for fourteen years," he says. "Fishing thousands of days and raising thousands and thousands of sailfish." But he could find very few fish over 100 pounds. The largest was 110.5 pounds—just a half pound shy of the record—which he caught in Golfito.

The big ones are simply no longer. "It's almost impossible to beat that record because they're not there to be caught. I'm not saying they're gone completely," Capozzi says. "But you can't find them in concentrations like they used to be." He points out that the world record black marlin was caught in the 1950s at a time when the location of massive schools of the fish was known around the world. "The Humboldt Current that created that is gone," he says. "The feed they ate—the anchovies—are gone."

Some of this he attributes simply to changes in the natural world—the Humboldt Current no longer funnels fish to a handy fishing hole—but he also thinks industrial fishing has had a profound impact.

"Commercial pressure has reduced the average weight of the fish around the world," he explains. In the Pacific sailfish he's hauled up off Costa Rica, Guatemala, and Venezuela, the decline has been significant. "Twenty or twenty-five years ago the average was probably eighty-five to ninety-five pounds. Nowadays, your average is sixty-five to seventy-five pounds. That's a gigantic difference."

"Besides," he says, "we're specialized mostly in light tackle."

For the Italian fisherman the challenge of landing a 175-pound fish on a fly line is sport enough. "You can see how challenging that is—it's the lightest line on the planet. It is very exciting . . . and very difficult."

Capozzi gets worked up describing the process of catching one of the biggest fish in the sea—on a fly. "Oh, it's a dance," he says. "You have to have it perfect, the presentation, the cast. . . . When it works it is a beautiful thing. You're fishing thirty-five feet from the stern and you can see it all happening. If that doesn't get you going, I don't know, go golfing."

●

Stacey Parkerson and Enrico Capozzi will continue to chase line-class records, particularly with the fly rod. As ever, the Italian has a whole list he'd like to best. And so does his lady angler. "I have several targets in mind in different locations around the world," she says. "Some are dreams and in far away locations, but that's what makes the fishing we do an exciting adventure."

Part of the fun is that adventure. Part of it is spending time out on the open seas. And a large component is simply besting the best.

"I love the challenge of it," says Parkerson, "knowing in my heart that I can do it.

"And proving to the boy's club that I can."

Enrico Capozzi, for one, is convinced.

"She's done things that have never been done in angling history, which is amazing to see. She's caught more billfish world records on the fly than any woman in history—and billfish are the most impressive fish."

CATCH AND RELEASE

A GOOD GAMEFISH IS TOO VALUABLE TO BE CAUGHT ONLY ONCE.
—LEE WULFF

W hen Greg Myerson sat down and thought about the striped bass that he'd killed to put his name in the world-record books, he felt terrible. He had quite a fight landing the eighty-three-pound creature, an exhausting tug of war that saw the former football star fall to the deck and take a hit that sent him to the emergency room. The striper was the biggest, most-impressive specimen of a species that he'd been chasing for decades, a catch that would surely win him the bass-fishing tournament in which he and his buddy were competing.

And yet something wasn't right.

"I really didn't want to keep it," he remembers, "because that fish was just beautiful."

Whether angling for big blue-water fish like marlin or for freshwater species like brown trout (as seen here), catch-and-release fishing is becoming increasingly urgent with the numbers of fishermen rising—and the populations of many species falling. The IGFA has recognized this urgency by adding a catch-and-release cat-

A lifelong outdoorsman, the burly Connecticut angler had developed a profound respect for the rockfish, and he found this particular catch had a big impact on him (even greater than the bruised rib he sustained).

"Something changed in me when I caught that fish," he says. "After killing that fish, I didn't feel like I had anything to prove. I'm not doing any more kill tournaments. I'll never kill another. It doesn't make me feel good."

Myerson was struck by the strength and power of the bass, and he imagined its history, defeating other fish in underwater turf wars and evading nets. "I killed a fish that had traveled all up and down the coast. That had lived a long life . . . and *survived*. So that victory was bittersweet for me."

Down in Florida, shark fisherman Bucky Dennis has had a similar crisis of conscience. He wished that he didn't have to kill the two big sharks he took to have them considered for world records. Dennis says he wouldn't have kept the big pregnant females if he wasn't concerned about the International Game Fish Association recognizing his record.

So he killed the massive beauties.

For decades, conservationists have been putting pressure on IGFA to change the requirements fishermen must meet to qualify for a world record, to relax standards just slightly so that visual documentation, measurements with approved tapes, and sworn testimony from witnesses would be good enough—and a fish could be put back in the water to swim again.

Just last year the organization made a big announcement. It's started an entirely new catch-and-release category. Now anglers can compete for world records for 127 species using a length-based methodology that doesn't require certified weights.

One of the early winners? Greg Myerson for striped bass.

●

Fishermen have been reeling in and releasing their quarry for more than a century. The practice was first documented in nineteenth-century Britain, where anglers were already concerned about dwindling populations of certain species. In the United States, famous fly-fisherman, conservationist, and outdoor writer Lee Wulff began to advocate for letting fish go in the 1930s. In a 1978 *Field & Stream* article he described showing films of himself "releasing game fish that were bigger than almost anyone in the audience had ever caught. There was shocked surprised—and very few cheers. Releasing good fish smacked of heresy."

Just two decades later attitudes were already changing. The notion of "fishing for fun"—as opposed to fishing for food—began to gain momentum. Many bodies of water were already showing signs of overfishing, and forward-thinking fishermen were beginning to see that they would have no fish to chase if things didn't change. In 1952, the State of Michigan established no-kill zones in some of its lakes to protect species. At the end of the decade, Trout Unlimited was formed by a group of Michigan anglers concerned with fish conservation, its history and philosophic underpinning rooted in the catch-and-release movement.

In the early days, catch-and-release thinking seemed associated entirely with freshwater species. It's not difficult for conservationists to prove that stock numbers are declining in a small basin or even a largish lake, and often fishermen can recognize problems simply by looking at their own success rates. But as study after study has shown offshore fish populations to be dwindling, too, deep-sea anglers have begun to adopt it as well. No-kill tournaments like Guy Harvey's Ultimate Shark Challenge in Florida are now not uncommon.

•

The phenomenon of fishing for big ones has remained a wrinkle, however. Even catch-and-release diehards will take a fish home for supper or the trophy case. And often these fish are the paragons of their populace, the ones that grow large and healthy and would make the finest families.

"By taking some of these females, we're wiping out all the best breeding stock," says striper fisherman Greg Myerson. Samantha Whitcraft, of the conservation organization Shark Savers, agrees. "What's important to note," she says, "is that it's the big females that are the most important to the future of the species."

"Fishermen often say, 'it's only one fish,'" she continues, using the hammerhead as an example. "But you're not just removing one fish, you're removing all of its future reproductive potential. It's way more than one fish. Every other year that fish can produce a litter of ten—and that's a conservative estimate—and if you figure she'll be reproducing for more than ten years, that's fifty fish. Granted, only one in ten survive, but that's still ten new fish in a species that's dwindling."

Florida shark fisherman Bucky Dennis does indeed make the argument that it was only one fish. Well, two. "I've only documented two in my life—for records," he says. And he's caught hundreds. "For the last ten years or so I average probably a dozen a year," he says. "Some seasons are better than others."

Fisherman Enrico Capozzi, who chases marlin and sailfish, says pretty much the same thing. "I've released more billfish than anyone in history—over ten thousand—and that is on light tackle, so the catches are not necessarily the largest specimen. I've kept maybe a dozen for world records. So percentage wise it's a really small amount."

Conservationists like Whitcraft would argue, yes, but the fish you kept were the big ones, the strongest most capable members of the species, the ones whose genes would be most beneficial to the future of their populations. But Bucky Dennis says that isn't the case. "The one I caught was 14.3 feet. I've had one on that's 17 to 18 feet long—I had a couple like that by the boat—and that would be close to two thousand pounds. I've had them bigger before."

●

Bucky Dennis says he would have been happy to let his two world-record sharks go—both pregnant females—if he could still win the world record. But IGFA doesn't allow that. "They have to be accurate," he says, so they require anglers to weigh their catches on certified scales on dry land. And as a competitive fishermen, he'll do what it takes to win.

"Catches can't be weighed on a boat, due to the rocking that may cause an inaccurate reading," says Jack Vitek, IGFA's world-record coordinator. He acknowledges the difficulty that poses for certain species.

"This prevents anglers targeting large offshore species (marlin, tuna, etc.) from releasing the fish alive."

And many big fish are not part of its new catch-and-release records. There are currently 1,322 all-tackle records to vie for, but only 167 catch-and-release categories. Samantha Whitcraft agrees that the world would be a better place if IGFA would change *all* of its rules.

"There is a lot out there now that makes catch and release viable for setting records. It's just that IGFA doesn't recognize it because they don't want to lose the older fishermen. Well, old fishermen are not the future. There are ways now—taking photographs, weighing on the boat—to record a record-breaking fish. The killing of these great big fish doesn't have to happen anymore. Wild fishing is not the future."

Jack Vitek says that the organization has felt the pressure. "The IGFA has received many requests from conservation-minded anglers and non-anglers alike, to develop new methods to determine world records . . . As a conservation-driven organization the IGFA is always looking for ways to reduce mortality and increase stocks for recreational anglers."

Enrico Capozzi praises the efforts of IGFA with the new category and adds, "They did it so more people will have access to world records," he says, "like kids and teenagers, who won't have to kill the fish and can avoid all the technicalities of line-class records." Plus he says, IGFA derives benefits, both through the publicity and good will it will receive and from fees it will derive from fisherman. "You have to pay for these record applications," he says. "Still, [the new catch-and-release program] it's a nice thing. A good thing."

Greg Myerson certainly thinks it's a good thing. He's added a second world record to his list of achievements and he seems as proud—perhaps even more so—of his catch-and-release record as he is of his all-tackle record.

He's not alone. Jack Vitek says a growing number of fishermen feel the same way. The large community of sportfishermen worldwide has embraced IGFA's new change. Of the 1,500 or so of the applications for world records that IGFA received in the past two years ("we usually get 700 to 750 a year," Vitek says) "just under half of all records (43 to 48 percent) were released alive."

Another bold step forward for the catch and release movement.

ACKNOWLEDGMENTS

Thanks go to my editor, Allen Jones, who has the patience of a fisherman.

Thanks also go to all the anglers I've profiled. The living ones all generously gave me their time, sent me photographs, and prodded me whenever I needed it—Greg Myerson, Bucky Dennis, Russell Jensen, Adam Konrad, Stacey Parkerson, Tom Healy, Roger Hellen, Patrick Keough, Enrico Capozzi. And thanks also to the support of Bill Baab, John Oliver, and all the other interviewees who made this book work. And to Jack Vitek of IGFA, who graciously offered me assistance at every turn.

Gratitude also goes to: my buddy Matthew Mayo, who helped me find this project and as ever gave me unerring advice, as he has steadfastly for years; my parents, who never got me into fishing but started me with a foundation to do what I do and continue to help me do it to this day; my wife, Lisa, who allows me to be my own Ahab, even if the source of my inspiration is the woods and the mountains rather than the deep; and my boys, Gus and Leo, who I hope will find something to love as much as the men and women on the preceding pages love to fish.

INDEX